# NARRATIVE APPROACHES TO YOUTH WORK

This is the book that youth workers who want to put into practice their desire to "meet youth where they're at" have been waiting for. *Narrative Approaches to Youth Work* provides hope-filled and fresh conversational practices anchored in a critical intersectional analysis of power and a relational ethic of care. These practices help youth workers answer the all-too-common question, *what do I do when I do youth work?* The concepts and skills presented in this book position youth workers to do youth work in ways that honor youth agency and resistance to oppression, invite a multiplicity of possibilities, and situate youth and youth workers alike within broader social contexts that influence their lives and their relationship together.

Drawing on the author's 30-plus years of working alongside young people and training youth workers in contexts ranging from recreation centers to homeless shelters, this book provides a rich and deliberate mix of theoretical grounding, practical application, real-life vignettes, and questions for in-depth self-reflection. Throughout *Narrative Approaches to Youth Work*, readers hear from a wise and thoughtful squad of youth workers talking about how they strive to do socially just, accountable, critical youth work.

**Julie Tilsen, PhD**, provides training and consultation for youth-serving agencies and teaches in the Youth Studies program at the University of Minnesota. She is the author of *Therapeutic Conversations with Queer Youth: Transcending Homonormativity and Constructing Preferred Identities.* Julie's work is featured in several professional training videos.

# NARRATIVE APPROACHES TO YOUTH WORK

## Conversational Skills for a Critical Practice

*Julie Tilsen*

Routledge
Taylor & Francis Group

NEW YORK AND LONDON

First published 2018
by Routledge
711 Third Avenue, New York, NY 10017

and by Routledge
2 Park Square, Milton Park, Abingdon, Oxon OX14 4RN

*Routledge is an imprint of the Taylor & Francis Group, an informa business*

© 2018 Taylor & Francis

*Library of Congress Cataloging-in-Publication Data*
Names: Tilsen, Julie Beth, 1962 – author.
Title: Narrative approaches to youth work: conversational skills for a
critical practice / Julie Tilsen.
Description: 1 Edition. | New York, NY: Routledge, 2018. | Includes
bibliographical references and index.
Identifiers: LCCN 2017044479 | ISBN 9781138091429 (hbk: alk. paper) |
ISBN 9781138091436 (pbk: alk. paper) | ISBN 9781315105970 (ebk)
Subjects: LCSH: Social work with youth. | Youth workers.
Classification: LCC HV1421 .T55 2018 | DDC 362.7—dc23
LC record available at https://lccn.loc.gov/2017044479

ISBN: 978-1-138-09142-9 (hbk)
ISBN: 978-1-138-09143-6 (pbk)
ISBN: 978-1-315-10597-0 (ebk)

Typeset in Bembo
by codeMantra

# CONTENTS

# FOREWORD

*Youth work* is an active and embodied form of praxis that exists at the intersections of informal education, care, therapeutic conversations, and social transformation. What distinguishes youth work from other human service work is the recognition that young people are always intended to be the primary beneficiaries (Sercombe, 2010). *Narrative approaches* are ways of working that draw on social constructionist and post-structural ideas to offer a unique way of thinking about persons and problems. Inspired by the visionary thinking of narrative therapy pioneers Michael White and David Epston (1990), narrative practitioners use language in fresh and creative ways to locate problems in social and historical contexts, instead of inside persons, and draw on young peoples' existing knowledge, wisdom, and skills to co-construct preferred identities and storylines. *Critical practices* are rooted in an awareness that many of the problems that young people face are not of their own making, but instead are rooted in historical and structural arrangements that benefit some groups at great cost to others. Critically oriented practitioners hold this in mind when working with young people and they take a stand against oppression in all its forms, in pursuit of a more just world (Aldarondo, 2007).

By bringing all these important strands together, Julie Tilsen shows the potency and relevance of conversational practices that are rooted in a stance of curiosity, appreciation, wonder, critical reflexivity, and incisive social and cultural critique. *Narrative Approaches to Youth Work: Conversational Skills for a Critical Practice* provides youth workers, students, educators and supervisors with a practical and theoretically robust approach to working with young people. Through a combination of stories, practice examples, reflective questions, and highly accessible descriptions of the theoretical traditions that inform this work, readers are provided with an up close view of youth work at its most gritty, tender, dialogical, and transformative.

Tilsen shows us that a narrative approach to youth work is not merely a set of skills, techniques, or decontextualized competencies to be mastered. Rather, she shows us that a narrative approach to youth work is a disciplined and artful form of praxis. It involves co-constructing meaning with young people to mobilize new understandings and create the conditions for them to live into preferred storylines and futures. Importantly, this type of youth work does *not* draw on the language of professional categories and expert knowledges (e.g. diagnostic labels) to understand and describe the lives of young people. On the contrary, it is an approach to practice that situates problems within a broad sociopolitical context and draws on creative conversational moves to challenge problem-saturated views and thin identity constructions (White & Epston, 1990). It is an exciting approach to practice that deeply resonates with the work of many of my Canadian colleagues who recognize youth work as politicized praxis (Loiselle et al., 2012; Reynolds, 2012; Saraceno, 2012; Skott-Myhre, 2006).

As the director of an academic program that is responsible for educating future youth workers in Canada, I deeply appreciate the way that this book offers youth workers, youth work supervisors, students, and educators such a compelling account of youth work for the twenty-first century. It is an approach that is relational, practical, theoretical, political, *and* responsive to the times we are currently living in (White, 2015). Here in North America, this includes reckoning with our own complicated embeddedness in colonial and racist histories and discourses, and becoming reflexive about our own sites of privilege and intersectional identities. This is a way of working that is deeply attuned to history, place, language, and relations of power, and it invites constant interrogation into how problems are constructed and the effects of these constructions on how we go on together.

*Narrative Approaches to Youth Work* offers a refreshing alternative to many existing textbooks in the human services/caring professions. On the one hand, we have texts that emphasize anti-oppressive practice frameworks without necessarily equipping youth workers with relational and conversational skills to support young people to pursue their preferred futures and become self-determining. On the other hand, we have texts that offer decontextualized "micro skills" (e.g. active listening, empathy, paraphrasing, open-ended questions), which rely quite heavily on individualistic, standardized frameworks and traditional psy-discourses, without offering any rigorous analyses of power, context, or history.

This book provides us with a both/and approach where questions are crafted to generate experiences (not just gather information) (Freedman & Combs, 1996), listening means attending to the unsaid and unsayable, and challenging unjust social structures is not considered outside the bounds of professional practice. Dr. Julie Tilsen draws on her decades of experience as a youth worker, therapist, educator, and social activist to bring youth work's critical, collaborative, playful, and revolutionary commitments and potentials to life.

Today, more than ever, we need what she calls a "scrappy, relationally-focused, youth-centered, intentionally political project."

— Jennifer White, School of Child and Youth Care,
University of Victoria, September 2017

## References

Aldarondo, E. (Ed.). (2007). *Advancing Social Justice through Clinical Practice*. Mahwah, NJ: Lawrence Erlbaum Associates.

Freedman, J., & Combs, G. (1996). *Narrative Therapy: The Social Construction of Preferred Realities*. New York, NY: Norton.

Loiselle, E., de Finney, S., Khanna, N., & Corcoran, R. (2012). "We need to talk about it!" Doing CYC as politicized praxis. *Child & Youth Services, 33*(3), 178–205.

Reynolds, V. (2012). An ethical stance for justice-doing in community work and therapy. *Journal of Systemic Therapies, 31*(4), 18–33.

Saraceno, J. (2012). Mapping whiteness and coloniality in the human service field: Possibilities for a praxis of social justice in child and youth care. *International Journal of Child, Youth & Family Studies, 3*(2/3), 248–271.

Skott-Myhre, H. (2006). Radical youth work: Becoming visible. *Child Youth Care Forum, 35*, 219–229.

Sercombe, H. (2010). *Youth Work Ethics*. Thousand Oaks, CA: Sage.

White, J. (2015). An ethos for the times: Difference, imagination, and the unknown future of child and youth care. *International Journal of Child, Youth, and Family Studies, 6*(4), 498–515.

White, M., & Epston, D. (1990). *Narrative Means to Therapeutic Ends*. New York, NY: Norton.

# ACKNOWLEDGMENTS

*Silent gratitude isn't very much use to anyone.*

Gladys Bronwyn Stern[1]

I find great pleasure in giving voice to gratitude after the arduous journey of book writing. It is a ritual of honoring connections and remembering my life with the people who have been there throughout the journey, but—when traveling down the lonely road of composition—it can be easy to lose sight of. *I see you*, each of you, for all the ways you touch and better my life.

To the scores of young people and youth workers I've crossed paths or rubbed elbows with over the years, for your stories full of struggle, wonder, hope, genius, and resistance... *I see you.*

To my editor at Routledge, Georgette Enriquez, and her assistant, Brian Eschrich, for jumping into this project eagerly, without hesitation, and for such great support... *I see you.*

To Scott Edelstein for some extra fine editing and agenting... *I see you.*

To Ray Lockman for being one badass and stubborn reference librarian... *I see you.*

To Katie Johnston-Goodstar and Jenna Sethi for engaging enthusiastically with me and my ideas while sharing a drink... or two... *I see you.*

To Clara Schiller and Jason Bucklin for conjuring and conceptual support with the book cover... *I see you.*

To Carys Cragg for reading, reflecting on, and resourcing this project all while you were in the final countdown to birth not only your own book, but also your human baby, John... *I see you*, and congrats!!

To my BFF Dave Nylund, and Sheila McNamee (the person-who-taught-me-everything-I-know), for generously reading every word of the emerging manuscript and providing the right brew of feedback, cheerleading, editing, suggestions, and emotional sustenance... *I see you.*

To Jennifer White for honoring this fan grrl with the gift of a perspicuous foreword for this little ditty, and for championing so many of the critical ideas that informs it...*I see you.*

To the youth workers—Jena Brune, Quinn Cordo, Jenna Dorschner, Eli Edelson-Stein, Angela Gauthier, Andrea Hite, Shanice "Sunnie" Mason, Mickella Rolfes, Val Rubin-Rashaad, Marjaan Sirdar, Emily Terrell, and Sam White—for their keen analyses, soul-full understandings, and fierce commitment to young people. I am so grateful for the generosity of your time and wisdom. Our conversations together, whether in my sunroom, at a coffee shop, or over Skype made me smile, touched my heart, and roused my passion... *I see y'all!*

To my love, Lauri, one wicked smart and clever youth worker in her own right, for insisting that I write this book... *I see you.* Now, let's go chase the Northern Lights.

## Note

1 Stern, G. B. (1954). *Robert Louis Stevenson, the man who wrote "Treasure Island": a biography.* New York, NY: Macmillan.

# INTRODUCTION

## Matching Your Practice with Your Intentions

> It is certain, in any case, that ignorance, allied with power, is the most ferocious enemy justice can have.
>
> *James Baldwin*

> If you listen for what you expect, it's dangerous.
>
> *Eli, a youth worker*

A few years ago, on the first day of the semester, a student asked me why I wanted to teach the course on youth work in the Youth Studies Program at the University of Minnesota.

Here is what I told the class:

> I continually witness youth workers who can articulate a thorough analysis of systems of oppression. Yet they struggle to interact with young people in ways that are anti-oppressive and that encourage youth agency. This struggle and disconnect makes sense to me; culturally, we're trained to communicate in certain ways, and embedded in these ways are the same operations of power that create and sustain the larger systems of oppression. It's understandable that youth workers—that all of us—bring these ways of communicating to our work.
>
> I'm teaching this class to offer some untraining, and to provide alternative ways of engaging that are coherent with a stand against oppression and for justice.

Just what was I talking about? What is this disconnect, and what do I suggest that we get untrained from—and trained into?

As a consultant and trainer, I talk with a lot of people who do all sorts of youth work in a variety of contexts. Overwhelmingly, they have a sophisticated analysis of systemic oppression and a passion for social justice. Most youth workers speak with conviction about young people's right to self-determination. They speak fluently about the effects on youth of white supremacy, patriarchy, heteronormativity, cisnormativity, classism, and other forms of institutional oppression. So, as I explained to my class, I'm generally impressed with the understanding that youth workers have of these broader systems, and I appreciate their intentions to do socially just work and support young people's agency.

Yet, when it comes down to their actual *engagement* with youth, their analyses and intentions often fail to inform the ways in which they interact with young people. What they understand on a systemic level and what they do in relationship with youth don't match up.

Said another way, many of the actual interactions youth workers have with young people unwittingly belie their resolve to promote youth agency and their desire to undo systems of oppression. Their relations with youth reflect— often subtly, sometimes not—normative ideas that lead workers to *give directives* rather than *invite possibilities*.

I am not the only one to notice this. Several critical scholar-practitioners in youth work (for example, Kouri, 2015; Pence & White, 2011; Skott-Myhre, 2006, 2008; White, 2007) note that the field has been overwhelmingly influenced by modernist discourses and practices—at the expense of cultivating a critical consciousness and knowledge of sociopolitical influences on young people's lives and the services we provide for them (Pence & White, 2011). The result of this, they argue (as do I), is that youth workers end up policing the borders of normativity, and they do not critically inquire about the effects of this policing on the young people they serve.

Put simply, youth workers end up becoming *The Man*—something no youth worker would ever aspire to be—effectively discouraging rather than encouraging youth self-determination.

That's where this book comes in: my intention is to help make the connection between where we stand politically—and by politically, I refer to power operations, not party affiliations—and ethically and how we work relationally. This book focuses on cultivating skills that are contextually situated and responsive. It will untrain you from typical ways of relating and train you into relational ways that support your intentions.

I often hear youth workers detail encounters with young people that lead to great frustration for both parties. Sometimes these experiences lead to disengagement from the relationship, loss of dignity for the young person, and self-doubt for the youth worker. This frustration comes from interactions fraught with adult, normative, and professional ideas (read: adult, white, middle-class) about what young people should do, what they need, and how they might best go about doing it or getting it. I hear stories narrated from a position of power and control; stories begging for attempts to understand and validate a youth's perspective; stories of youth workers who are quick to tell and slow to listen; and stories that fail to account for the social/cultural/political contexts that influence not only the young person, but also the engagement between them and the youth worker.

In short, I hear:

1. Stories told from a position informed by our individualist/patriarchal culture that demands personal responsibility while denying the limiting effects of systems of power
2. Stories contaminated with notions of "normal" and "appropriate," generated from the social service/psychiatric/prison industrial complex, and intoxicated by the free-flowing rhetoric of psychopathology
3. Stories told by people who aren't sure how to engage from a philosophical stance other than individualism

Please understand, I am absolutely *not* saying that I hear stories from mean, uncaring, disinterested, oppressive, youth-despising, stupid adults employed as youth workers. On the contrary, I'm saying that I hear these stories from kind, loving, passionate, justice-seeking, youth-affirming, bright people who serve youth, but who haven't been given the necessary concepts or conversational practices and skills. They have the best of intentions and the requisite knowledge about social systems of oppression, but they lack the resources for working and conversing with young people.

As an example, here is an exchange that a youth worker at a transitional housing program shared with me:

> YW: So, four youth were in the commons area playing cards, just loud and carrying on, you know, giving each other the business while they were playing. There were other youth hanging out there, talking and using the computer or whatnot. It's like they were playing cards on their own planet, not thinking about anyone else there, the other residents. So I went up to them and said, "Hey, you guys, you're being super disrespectful to everyone else. Please use this space in a way that doesn't keep others from using it, too, or you'll lose your privileges." Then they went OFF. "You can't take commons privileges from us! We live here! We're just having fun—no one is complaining except you! You think you run this place, but we live here; you just work here!" I told them that getting salty with me wasn't going to help, that I was asking them nicely just to be quiet. I said, "It doesn't have to be a big deal, you know." It just kept going from there...

Indeed. Power struggles do generally just keep going.

What else could this youth worker have done? What approach or position could she have taken that would have engaged the four cardplayers in a way that (1) led to the youth worker and the four young people sharing a purpose, rather than squaring off with differing purposes; (2) maintained the dignity of everyone involved; (3) demonstrated an understanding of what mattered to the young people; (4) cultivated a richer connection between the youth worker and residents; and (5) achieved a commons area arrangement that allowed all residents to use it in multiple ways?

As we will see, there is a great deal that this youth worker might have done differently. This book is about such alternative approaches—all in the context of everyday interactions and conversations.

*Narrative Approaches to Youth Work* presents a wide range of conceptual and conversational resources, all based on social constructionist philosophy, post-structural theory, and narrative practices. These expand the meaningful and productive ways in which youth workers can engage youth, while honoring young people's self-determination, skills, and knowledges. They represent some of the most innovative and distinctive contributions to relationally oriented work that have emerged over the last 30 years.

These ideas embody youth work at its best: a mutually influential, unpredictable yet safe, creatively improvised yet intentionally cultivated, liberatory partnership. This partnership focuses on young people's preferences, hopes, and imaginations through a relational engagement of curiosity and responsiveness. And pizza, of course. Every good youth worker knows that there always has to be pizza.

I want to be clear: this is not a "survey" book that summarizes several theories and techniques from a variety of approaches, many of which are theoretically inconsonant with each other. Instead, the concepts and practices in this book are firmly and intentionally positioned within the philosophical paradigm of social construction, with a particular emphasis on ideas and practices that have emerged from the interdisciplinary body of work that constitutes narrative approaches. (Don't worry if you don't know what these terms mean; those are some of the things this book is here to teach you!)

## Not Just for Problems

You may be wondering if the ideas contained in this book are only useful with "at-risk" youth, with young people facing problems in their social world (e.g. academic difficulties, involvement with the justice system, homelessness, etc.), or with youth who struggle under the burdens of racism, economic injustice, patriarchy, heteronormativity, cissexism, ableism, and other forms of systemic oppression. The answer in all cases is an emphatic *no*. As you will discover, the tools and skills provided here can assist youth workers with *all* young people, in all sorts of contexts. These tools and skills can help you have generative, creative, hope-filled conversations that leverage young people's imaginations, knowledge, abilities, hopes, and intentions.

These ideas and practices speak to the heart of what youth work strives to be: a relational practice that leverages young people as resources for influence and change in their own lives and communities. They also reflect the soul of a good youth worker: someone who can see in each young person the potential and possibilities that most others are blind to.

## The Consultant's Consultants

Throughout this book, you will find comments from a variety of youth workers who served as consultants to the creation of this volume. Their comments, excerpted from several conversations, offer insider perspectives that can help anchor the ideas presented here to the lived experiences of youth workers. Our discussions focused on how they think about things like engagement and relationship, and what they actually *do* when they say they're *doing youth work*.

Below is a brief introduction (in their own words) to each of the youth workers who generously provided their time and knowledge:

**Jena Brune:** "I'm a white, cis, able-bodied woman who loves the art of connection. I have two decades of experience using conversation, visual and performing art, curiosity, and accountability to guide collaboration with youth. In my work, I try to use 'Be there. Be honest. Be on it' as a compass. I partner with youth experiencing homelessness to define and activate their own learning goals in ways that feel most meaningful to them."

**Quinn Cordo:** "I think I've probably been doing youth work since I was a young person. Feeling devalued because of my age compelled me to advocate for myself and others. One of the most important takeaways from my experiences with youth is that young people are capable, but they often lack the opportunities and resources that help them live into their abilities. I aspire to cocreate with young people the change they want to see in their lives. I'm a queer, Jewish, white, cisgender-ish/agender-ish, able-bodied, middle-class male."

**Jenna Dorschner:** "As a child, I always knew that I wanted to work with youth in some capacity. I am most passionate about mental health and working toward ending the stigma and prejudice imposed upon youth who struggle with their mental health. I have worked with youth in a variety of settings including day camps and youth circuses. I enjoy cocreating relationships that promote trust and understanding. I'm a cis, straight, white woman."

**Eli Edleson-Stein:** "I grew up in the Jewish communities of the Bay Area and Minneapolis. I'm a white, queer, Jewish, cisgender male. My youth work practice is rooted in a constant play between listening, questioning, and contextualizing relationships inside of systems of power. I believe in platitudes and science fiction: young people are the future!"

**Angela Gauthier:** "I began working with youth experiencing homelessness in 2006. Since 2007, I have been learning how to be a white ally through my work in the American Indian community. I work as a program director, overseeing programming focused on Indian Child Welfare (ICWA), cultural teaching, family advocacy, transitional living, and emergency shelter for youth, mental health case management, and therapy services. I'm a queer, cis, able-bodied woman."

**Andrea Hite:** "I'm a Korean-American adoptee who was raised in the great state of Minnesota and currently reside in Chicago. I'm an extroverted-introvert who loves dogs, learning by doing, and helping people identify their super powers. I'm a staunch believer in self-care, bubble baths, and diet coke."

**Shanice "Sunnie" Mason:** "I'm always surprised to see what youth harbor inside themselves—there's so much potential that can be fostered once it's revealed. When I can provide space to help a young person realize that they are not their circumstances, it's a profound experience, not only for the youth, but also for me. I do my best to be the trusting adult that I needed in my life when I was young. I'm a cis-female, demisexual, African-American."

**Mickella Rolfes:** "I was kicked out of my house when I was a teenager. Now I work with youth teaching resilience and resistance. I've worked with toddlers and infants who are in precarious and, at times, violent situations, as well as with young adults fighting incarceration. I collaborate with probation officers, public defenders, county judges, and even the police, advocating for young people, challenging systemic racism, and fighting for criminal justice reform. I'm a straight, cisgender, white, able-bodied woman."

**Val Rubin-Rashaad:** "I'm from a rural area and I had pet chickens growing up. Since 1990, I've worked in shelters, done street outreach, facilitated youth leadership programs, and provided advocacy and case management services. I specialize in sexual health education, HIV prevention, and telling hilarious stories. I'm a straight, black, able-bodied mom and a grandma, and I always have condoms with me. Youth work is my calling and I try to approach it with humility... and humor."

**Marjaan Sirdar:** "I'm a straight, cis, Black man who grew up in a low-income, single-parent home in suburban Minneapolis, attending predominantly white schools and feeling invisible. I never had any teachers of color or positive Black men in my life. This experience inspired me to work with youth. I worked with homeless youth for seven years before becoming a teacher. My goals include helping youth unlearn the dominant narrative of white supremacy and use education as a means of liberation."

**Emily Terrell:** "I have worked alongside youth as a coach, youth ministry leader, and counselor in settings ranging from high schools to shelters, juvenile justice programs to community clinics. My husband and I mentor a phenomenal young man who, at 16 years old, was our Best Man. I'm a straight, white, cis, able-bodied, Harry Potter fangirl, and I like making multicolored friendship bracelets and coloring. I debrief a hard day with Mary J. Blige."

**Sam White:** "I am a bi/queer black woman from the East Coast. I've also put down temporary roots in France, Brazil, and China. I feel most at home when I am outside and enjoy connecting young folks with opportunities to engage in nature and outdoor recreation. I am driven by tenderness, compassion, and a fierce sense of justice. My self-care practice looks like running, walking, and making meals for myself and others."

What about me? I'm a queer, cisgender, Jewish, over-50 woman who walks through the world with the unearned privileges afforded to those with: white skin, bodies that conform to most normative specifications, a US birth certificate, an advanced degree, and a stable income. I was kicked out of day camp when I was six because the adults thought I asked too many questions. I wrote a manifesto in seventh grade in which I suggested several significant changes teachers should make in their relationships with students as well as their pedagogy, and I turned down an invitation to join the National Honor Society in high school because I thought it was elitist and failed to "honor" all the students who deserved it. And I like women's hockey. *A lot.*

## Moving Beyond What You Know Now

*"People do what they know."* Years ago, a young person said this to me at a drop-in center. She said it as she witnessed an interaction gone bad between one of the center staff and two other young people. I asked her if she would tell me more about what she meant. She said, referring to the youth worker, "He didn't mean them any harm. He just told them the rules—that's what he tells everyone—'cuz that's really all he knows to do."

That comment—*people do what they know*—has stayed with me over the years. Whenever I feel stuck and unable to keep a conversation going in a generative and hopeful way, I wonder what else I might be able *to know* about relating to and engaging with others.

This book offers concepts and practices informed by social construction and post-structural theories that are intended to help you continually expand what you know. These are *doing with*, not *doing to*, practices. They are practices that are theoretically and ethically in line with the aspirations of youth work: youth engagement, youth agency, and youth self-determination.

The book is organized into three parts. Part I centers on the theoretical foundations and organizing concepts of social construction that inform the practice of youth work. Part II is organized around a critical integration of theory and practice, or praxis. You will find specific narrative ideas and skills to integrate into your youth work practice in these chapters. In Part III, I make an earnest request of you to take your commitment to young people and the practice of youth work beyond the bounds of your daily interactions.

Chapters 1 and 2 introduce you to the theoretical foundations that inform this work. I discuss social construction and post-structural theory as alternatives to the conventional Western worldview on identity, language, power relations, and communication that permeate our social interactions, both within and outside of youth work practice. These concepts—of discourse and discursive production, essentialist vs. non-essentialist identities, the narrative metaphor, and positioning—serve as the conceptual footing for the practices that follow.

Although often compartmentalized away from the whole of practice, ethics is at the center of all our work. In Chapter 3, I discuss ethics as a relational stance, not a tactical response to a dilemma or a codified set of guidelines to help us avoid legal trouble. Relational ethics and an ethic of care are central to a socially just practice that is flexible, responsive, and contextual.

Chapters 4–6 dive into the heart of relational engagement: listening, understanding, asking questions, making meaning, and collaborative storying. This is what youth workers and youth *do together*. These chapters address some very big ideas by unpacking them and breaking them down for you to practice and integrate into your work.

Chapter 7 focuses on question asking. While theory provides the grounding, and listening and meaning making serve as the soul of this practice, it is the craft of asking questions that gives conversations form. This form allows conversations to move through time and space, from problems to possibilities, and into the expansive dimensions of hope, wonder, and creativity.

Chapter 8 focuses on relational and language practices for talking about and addressing problems that often enter young people's lives. I introduce externalizing conversations as a practice that brings forward youth agency, invites accountability, and prevents the collapse of problem stories onto their identities.

Pop culture is youth culture, and we really can't expect to have meaningful connections with young people if we don't have meaningful ways of connecting with them around pop culture. Thus, Chapter 9 presents some methodologies from the interdisciplinary field of cultural studies. These approaches go hand in hand with the concepts and skills provided elsewhere in this book. They also provide youth workers with approaches to inquiry that can help young people take a critical look at their relationship with the products of the media industries.

Chapter 10 addresses how becoming an effective youth worker is an ongoing process. This chapter encourages you to take up the project of becoming your very best at engaging effectively with young people. In it, you walk through strategies for a deliberate, reflexive practice that will help you cultivate your capacity for engaging with more young people in more varied and more effective ways.

Throughout this book, I closely examine the politics and effects of power operations on each topic I address. Chapter 11, the concluding chapter, extends this examination a step further, beyond the relational bounds of youth worker-young person engagement. In this chapter, we look at the broader sphere of community organizing and activism as an aspect of youth work, and invite you to consider the place of activism in youth work practice.

As you read, you'll find questions for reflection—and, often, for encouraging deconstruction and meaning making. I also offer some brief scenarios for you to consider—and to discuss with colleagues, fellow students, your supervisor, or possibly some young people. Most of these involve interactions between youth workers and young people that I've experienced or that other youth workers have shared with me. Be careful not to take any of these as the one right way to approach similar situations; consider each one as simply one way that the conversational resources presented in this book were used.

Lastly, I have included #FergusonSyllabus[1] questions for each chapter. These questions, organized around the main theme of each chapter, invite you to consider the chapter material in terms of power relations and broader cultural issues. In particular, these questions focus on the implications of doing youth work within the context of white supremacy/racism, patriarchy/misogyny, heteronormativity/heterosexism, capitalism/classism, cisnormativity/transphobia, and other such oppressive cultural norms.

Youth work has a rich history of theory, pedagogy, research, and practice. In writing this book, I join other scholars/practitioners/educators/activists who have called for conceptual and conversational resources from post-structural theory and constructionist philosophy to be embraced by the field of youth work. These ideas and practices are already widely used in community work, healthcare, education, psychotherapy, leadership and organizational development, research, conflict management, mediation, and so forth.

The ideas and practices in this book have been helpful to the youth work professionals and students I've shared them with, and they form the center of my own practice as a youth worker, educator, consultant, and researcher. I invite you to discover what they are, what's different about them, and why they should matter to you and other youth workers. As you'll see, these concepts and practices will be much more than just a good fit with youth work philosophy. They will help you bring to life the intentions of all great youth workers: to honor young people's agency, support their right to self-determination, and create opportunities for them to share their genius with the world.

## Note

1  Georgetown University history professor Marcia Chatelain created #FergusonSyllabus in 2014. She wanted to encourage educators to address issues raised following the murder of Michael Brown by local police in Ferguson, MO. The Twitter hashtag was used by educators to crowdsource and share materials and ideas for bringing discussions of the events into classrooms. In my own course, I created a #FergusonSyllabus question for each class topic.

# PART I

# Philosophical Groundwork for Relationally Engaged Youth Work

> But if theory is not the crystallized resin of experience, it ceases to be a guide to action.
>
> *Leslie Feinberg*

> I have to reflect and think about what I did, write it down, and ask "what drives that and what did it do?"
>
> *Andrea, a youth worker*

Do not skip this stuff. Please.

One of the challenges of our drive-through, Snapchat, 140-character culture is that we often jump into *doing* stuff without considering (1) what ideas are behind and beneath the doing, (2) where those ideas come from, and (3) what those ideas and the doing of them create, or result in.

In youth work practice, this often ends up manifesting in youth workers asking colleagues and supervisors to "just tell me what to do." That approach is, by definition, unrelational and insufficient. At times, we all find ourselves desperately searching for the magic words that will help us turn a rough corner with a young person. There are, of course, no such words. Any magic emerges from the relationship and the interaction, not the speaking of silver-bullet words.

Furthermore, we are less likely to search for "what to do" when we are grounded in concepts and conversational resources that create genuine engagement, when we organize our work around a relational ethic, and when we maintain a reflexive practice in which we continually ask critical questions about our work. The chapters in Part I lay the foundation for all these activities. They also position ethics at the center of youth work.

We are always influenced by certain ways of understanding the world, whether we are aware of it or not, and whether or not we can articulate any of those ways. This is not bad, it is simply inevitable. The point is to be intentional about which philosophical stance you take and to stay reflexively engaged with what comes from that.

The first three chapters of this book invite you to take a particular stance when doing youth work. The concepts introduced in this part provide the conceptual framework for the specific practices provided in Parts II and III. This framework functions as your conversational compass for the relational paths of possibility you will travel with the young people you work with. Don't head out without a working compass.

# 1

# WHERE YOU COMING FROM?
# A PHILOSOPHY FOR THE PRACTICE
# OF YOUTH WORK

> The engaged voice must never be fixed and absolute but always changing, always evolving in dialogue with a world beyond itself.
>
> *bell hooks*

> I went to talk with him and I didn't have any idea where the conversation would go.
>
> *Quinn, a youth worker*

Why do we need a philosophy or theory to inform our work? Can't we *just talk* to youth?

When youth workers express this sentiment, or others like it, I'm reminded of the story about the fish that is asked how the water is. The fish responds, "Water? What's that?"

Like the fish that has always known—and only known—a particular context and a certain way of being, we are often unaware that when we "just talk," that talk comes from a particular philosophical framework—and that philosophy is reflected in our talk.

In fact, *some* philosophical/cultural framework always informs any social/relational activity. Each framework puts forth ideas about how to be in the world. It's impossible to "just talk" without having the talking we do—our words, our assumptions, our intentions, our understanding of ourselves and those we're talking to—reflect the assumptions and ideas of some philosophical framework. Because that philosophy is all around us and it's all we've known, we just do it. (And often, like the fish, we have no conscious recognition of it.) These frameworks are society's lenses through which we interpret the world. The realities that we take for granted are the realities in which we are immersed.

In contemporary North American culture, the guiding framework that informs many of our social activities is individualism[1]. Individualism leads to a certain kind of talk. Conversations within the framework of individualism are often thought of as transmitting information from one person to another, or as an exchange of information. Language is thought of as describing truths, and often we end up trying to convince others of The Truth—as we see it.

Within an individualist framework, social/relational complexities and context go largely overlooked in favor of a focus on what goes on "inside" of individual persons. Our attention is given to what is one's "authentic self," what is "in their heads" or "in their hearts." With our interest solidly placed in this idea of *interiority* (that is, the stuff "inside" of people), all our efforts to shape, change, inspire, or otherwise influence others are directed at people's "insides."

That's not where I'm coming from. When I mentioned the idea of untraining in the introduction, I was referring to helping you get untrained from individualism.

## Language as Action

Conversations should take youth to a new place.

*Angela, a youth worker*

The ideas and practices in this book are informed by social construction, a philosophical stance that is relational rather than individual. When we take a social constructionist stance, we understand language and what it does very differently than we do within the discourse[2] of individualism. To begin with, social construction understands language not as descriptive, or as a means to convey undisputed facts about an assumed reality; rather, language is a relational process of *making meaning.*

For example, when I say, "I'm sitting at my desk writing, looking out the window at the trees," what my language *makes* doesn't stop at the description I offer. You are assigning meaning, and what you come up with may be very different from what I'm experiencing. As a result, your interpretation—and the significance you make—of my words are likely to be very different than mine.

A lot depends on your relationship with trees, writing, desks, and sitting, as well as on the many cultural factors that influence you. What does *sitting at my desk writing* mean, if anything, in your experience and culture? What kinds of trees grow where you live? Is *desk* a term for a concept that represents something to you? What does *my desk* mean, and what sense of relationship or ownership do those words convey to you?

Even the temporal dimension of your experience shapes the meaning you make. Would you have assigned the same meaning or significance to that sentence last year? Will its meaning change for you over time?

There are also personal considerations that influence meaning. Have you had any especially important experiences involving trees, desks, or writing?

Thus, we shift from a visual metaphor, where language describes the observable, to a dialogic metaphor, in which *language produces meaning*. Language is productive, not merely descriptive or reflective. In social construction, this is known as *discursive production*—that is, the making of discourse.

---

## Social Construction: From Noun to Verb

You may be familiar with the idea of *social constructs*. For example, it's common to hear that race and gender are social constructs. This means that the existence of race and gender are determined by the introduction, imposition, and acceptance of such concepts by culturally influential groups. There is nothing universal or natural about race or gender; their meanings change across time and place.[3]

But how does this happen? How do social constructs come to be? And if they're created in the social world, how do they have such real effects on people? That is the focus here: the *process* of social construction.

A helpful way to think about this is to shift from the static nouns of *constructs* to the dynamic verb of *constructing*. Thus, we are not only interested in any given construct and the meanings associated with it; we are also very much focused on *how* people participate in the process of socially constructing the meanings.

---

By acknowledging that language is productive rather than merely descriptive, we now see how notions of "truth" and "reality" begin to come unhinged: if you and I cannot assume the same understanding of *desk, tree, writing*, or *sitting*, there is little room to claim universal agreement on what is true and real. In this way, social construction is skeptical of universal truths applied to all people, regardless of the context. (Universal truths are a hallmark of modernist discourse, the worldview of individualism.) This skepticism comes to life through questioning *what* we know, as well as of *how* we came to know it, and *whom* such knowledge might benefit. This process of questioning is known as *deconstruction* (Derrida, 1967, 1977).

Instead of a singular, ostensibly objective view of reality, social construction views reality as multiple, subjective, and historically and culturally contingent. This view of language shifts the emphasis from individualism and from language as a representation of a singular reality, to a set of social activities shared between and among people who partner as agents of the production of multiple realities (Wittgenstein, 1953).

What does this mean in youth work? For one, it means that we have to work very hard to understand and attend to young people's meanings as they share their experiences. (We will go more deeply into listening for understanding, meaning making, and validating meaning in later chapters.) It also means that we need to be self-reflexive: we may need to interrupt ourselves when we (wittingly or unwittingly) impose our meanings, or those of the prevailing culture and discourses, on young people.

This process of exposing and deconstructing discursive assumptions is central to constructionist philosophy and narrative practice. These assumptions, which reflect the dominant discourses (and which are often organized around ideas of what is "right," "appropriate," or "normal"), serve to colonize youth into dominant or normative ways of being. They also close off untold other ways of making meaning and taking action in the world.

Understanding that language *does things* also means that a whole world of possibilities opens up when we enter collaborative conversations with young people. Because *meaning is always on the way* (McNamee, personal communication), the productive potential of language can be leveraged through generative conversations with young people.

One other critical principle of social construction is that all this meaning making isn't happening "in your head" in a completely individualistic process. Instead, meaning making is a social process through which people negotiate meaning together.[4] So, even if you're up in your head envisioning desks, trees, and writing right now, the experiences you've had with those things, and the meanings you've established for them, came from the social world. They haven't been in your brain since birth, nor did they "develop" there because you're a certain age. And, right now, because you and I are considering all of this together, we're negotiating meaning in the social world via this book.

## Making Me from the Outside In: Implications for Identity

> Youth work is identity work.
>
> *Marjaan, a youth worker*

Youth work concerns itself a great deal with young people's identity development. Indeed, helping youth "develop" is an implicit, and often explicit, intention of all youth work.

However, when we take a constructionist stance and accept that meaning is relationally produced, we must reject another firmly held assumption of individualism: the idea of the self-contained individual. This assumption holds that a person's identity is determined by their *essence,* what is supposedly inside of them. This essential self is understood to be fixed and stable.

The pervasiveness of essentialist notions of identity is readily visible in the use of clichés such as *authentic self, true self,* and *just be yourself.*[5]

In contrast to the essentialized *self* of individualism, social construction privileges the notion of *identity* as embodying multiple fluid and emergent qualities. Identity shifts through time and in context. For each of us, there are possibilities for a variety of identities, each dependent on context. As Burr (2003) notes, identity is a social concept and a social *act*:

> When you identify something, say a plant or an animal, you give it an identity. To say "that's a weed" or "there's a wild animal" is not to detect some essential feature of nature of the thing you're looking at. "Flower" versus "weed" is a dimension only relevant if you are a gardener. "Edible" versus "inedible" might be the unarticulable dimension used by sheep and cows. And "wild" versus "tame" is a distinction that surely only has meaning for humans, since "tame" implies an encounter and relationship with human beings. The point is that it is you that is doing the identifying, and the identity you confer has more to do with your purposes than the nature of the thing itself.
>
> (p. 106)

Of course, people aren't plants or farm animals. Yet this process of identifying others and ourselves is something we habitually do. Consider just some of the identity categories that we acknowledge among (or impose upon) the young people we work with (as well as others we encounter):

- Gender
- Race
- Class
- Nationality
- Sexuality
- Ability
- Religion
- Citizenship status
- Culture or ethnicity

These are all categories that we may take for granted as so-called natural identities (some more so than others). But as Foucault (1965, 1977, 1982) suggests in his analysis of power, these are all manufactured through powerful discursive practices.[6] Discourses circulating through culture effectively institutionalize what identities are available to us. Furthermore, these identities gain meaning in relationship to others. This underscores the notion that meaning is negotiated relationally. For example, *man* gains meaning in relationship to *woman*, and *transgender* gains meaning in relationship to *cisgender*.

In this way, instead of affirming an individual, fixed interior self, constructionists hold that "identity becomes the accomplishment of situated activity" (McNamee, 1996, p. 150). Relationships are the situated activity. As relational constructs, identities are *stories* about ourselves. Some of these stories affect us in preferred ways, while others are problematic.

---

### #FergusonSyllabus Question

How does understanding youth identity as culturally contingent, flexible, and emergent generate possibilities for new ways of being, even within discourses that seek to specify and marginalize young people?

What does this make possible for youth of color? For girls and young women? For gender nonconforming youth? For young people whose identities are scrutinized because of their culture, physical ability, economic status, gender, sexuality, and/or ethnicity?

---

### What About the Physical World?

What about someone with a disability or chronic illness? Isn't that an example of a *natural* identity? How is, for example, the identity of a youth on the Autism Spectrum socially constructed? Isn't that a physical fact about that young person?

Social construction doesn't deny the physical world. However, it acknowledges that the ways the physical world *is understood* are culturally and historically contingent. The descriptions used and stories told about illness and disease—even what gets to be *considered* an illness or disease—can vary in different contexts and at different times.

For example, some young people are neuro-nonconforming; that is, they experience and relate to the social world in ways that are not typical of how most people do. Thus, we tell different stories about them and we use different language to describe them.

Youth work informed by social construction is interested in helping young people avoid *totalizing* descriptions of themselves based only on the disability or disease that impacts them. (I'll say more about totalizing descriptions in Chapter 2.)

---

## Implications for Youth Work

> Skills are attached to identities; youth can export skills from one identity to another.
>
> *Mickella, a youth worker*

What does this shift from self to identity make possible? How is this useful in youth work?

First, when we shift from something that is static and stable to something that is flexible and emergent, new identities become possibilities to consider. When we move to *identity from the outside in*, limitations or problematic identities become stories that youth can be in relationship with. They (and we) can then examine their effects and consider revising those stories.

We make sense of the world through stories; indeed, identities are stories about ourselves, circulated both by others and by ourselves. (This includes our circulating of stories when we are in silent conversation with ourselves.) A young person is not stuck with an identity they have inside of them or with something they may have to grow into or develop. Instead, they can explore what their intentions and preferences are, and cultivate practices for living into them. Similarly, when a young person lives into an identity that suits them— say, for example, a "good team player"—we can engage them in a rich conversation about why that matters, how they live into it, who supports them in it, what they hope will come from it, etc. In effect, we help them author a story about the meaning of being a good team player.

Thus, moving from self to identity is a move from essence to story (Tilsen, 2013). In turn, this makes possible another shift: from asking the question *Who are you?* to asking, *Who would you like to be?*[7] As we will see, this question alone leads to many other questions that generate conversations rich in possibilities.

## Identities in the World: Stories Within Stories

> It's about what stories are being told about them, and how little we allow youth to contextualize their experiences.
>
> *Emily, a youth worker*

We need to consider one more concept that is fundamental to a constructionist worldview: our individual stories are embedded within, and influenced by, guiding cultural narratives or discourses. Brace yourself, because what I'm about to write is in direct opposition to something the individualist worldview teaches us to hold near and dear to us:

> *We are not the authors of our own stories.* That is, we are not the *only* authors of our own stories. We don't—and can't—have total editorial authority.

Individualism tells you to "be your own person," no matter what is going on around you. Social construction suggests instead that, no matter what any of us does, we can never define ourselves outside of the prevailing discourses, beyond the boundaries of the culture's meta-narratives. Even identities that differ from dominant identities (steampunk, transgender, or disabled, for example) are defined *in relationship to* the prevailing discourses. *Steampunk* gains distinction in relation to *advanced technology*; *transgender* gains distinction in relation to *cisgender*; *disabled* gains distinction in relation to *able-bodied*.

When we conceptualize a nonessential self, our identities gain meaning in relationship to the available discourses that operate in our contexts. This is because discourses regulate and specify what texts or stories are available for personal narratives.

For example, let's consider a cisgender male who plays high school football. What are the cultural stories, or discourses, available for his identity? Dominant masculinity is an obvious discourse that is hugely influential in the lives of young cisgender men, and potentially more so for football players. People may make meaning of this identity by believing him to be disrespectful to women, insensitive, inclined to use violence, and entitled. Further, the discourse of dominant masculinity has traditionally demanded that he be not only straight, but also outwardly homophobic. These are stories we tell ourselves and each other about this person.

Then, when this particular young man brings his boyfriend to prom, joins the Gay-Straight Alliance (GSA),[8] and marches with the queer youth group in the Gay Pride Parade—all while breaking conference records as a star running back—he may be lauded as a "brave and courageous queer youth." This is another story—another common discourse—that we tell ourselves and each other about this young man: that being queer *and* a football player requires courage in a homophobic context of dominant masculinity.

Yet if our culture were not already heavily under the influence of discourses about football players, then an out, GSA-attending, Pride-marching football star wouldn't carry a great deal of meaning. Because of those prevailing discourses, however, this young person's performance of resistant[9] identities gains great meaning. If we don't acknowledge and examine the cultural discourses and meta-narratives that help to shape individual stories, we suck some of the meaning out of these personal accounts of identity and we ignore how power operates in the social world.

## Summary

Social construction offers youth workers a philosophical stance that aligns with the liberatory intentions of the field of youth work. With its focus on the relationship among discourse, power, and identity, social construction provides the conceptual groundwork for encouraging generative, honoring, and hope-filled engagements with young people.

The shift from individualism to social construction means a shift from one kind of talk to another. This is a shift from a language that transmits information, describes the "truth," and attempts to convince to a language that produces meaning, honors multiple truths, and seeks to understand.

# Highlights

## *Principles of Individualism vs. Social Construction*

|  | *Individualism* | *Social Construction* |
|---|---|---|
| Key Metaphor | Visual; observing structures | Dialogic; producing meaning |
| Truth | Singular, objective, universal | Multiple, subjective, local, contingent |
| Reality | Singular, objective, observable | Multiple, subjective, discursively produced |
| Language | Describes the "real" world<br>Transmission of facts | Produces meaning<br>Discursive production |
| Identity | The self: authentic, internal, natural, fixed, essential | Constructed, constituted relationally, contingent, emerging, multiple |
| Relation to the Social World | Autonomy, individuated | Individual stories gain meaning within cultural narratives and discourses |

## Key Terms

1. **Deconstruction:** A process used to understand text[10] in context and to expose taken-for-granted assumptions embedded within it. Deconstruction operates on the assumption that nothing exists outside of text and that there is no objective reality that has meaning outside of the context(s) that give it meaning. Derrida (1967) is closely associated with deconstruction.

2. **Discourse:** Foucault (1970) defines discourse as a "social practice" that circulates through culture. Discourse has a regulating effect on what may or may not be spoken. We cannot speak, think, feel, or act free from the influence of discourse. Even resistance and transgressions gain their meaning through their relationship to discourse. Discourse is what gets to be said, who gets to say it, with what authority, and with what effects.

3. **Discursive production:** In social construction, language is understood to be productive, not merely descriptive. That is, language does things. Discursive production occurs when meanings and ideas are made and circulated such that they create an understanding that is shared.

4. **Essentialism:** Essentialism asserts that specific core (or "essential") characteristics or properties are shared by all members of a particular group, regardless of the context. Essentialist identities (conceptualized within the worldview of modernism/individualism) are those identities that are thought to be "authentic" and "natural," and are part of a person's internal world.

5. **Individualism:** Individualism is a cornerstone of modernist philosophy and liberal humanism; it is related to essentialism. It promotes the notion of a self-contained, unique, essentialized, "authentic" self.

6.  **Social construction:** A philosophical stance that focuses on language practices (what occurs among people) rather than on observation of structures (what is ostensibly inside of people). Constructionist philosophy stands in opposition to individualism, modernism, and essentialism.

## Discussion Questions

1.  Describe your own current philosophical stance on youth work.
2.  How does the idea that language is productive show up in our day-to-day lives? What are some examples of this?
3.  What are some of your own identities—e.g. the stories about yourself—that you and others tell? What discourses influence these personal identities and narratives? What are the effects of these discourses on you? On others?
4.  What are some common discourses about youth that you can recognize and articulate?

## Notes

1  For more on individualism, and the cultural contexts and ideas that shape it, see Sampson (2008).
2  Discourse refers to how power flows through culture, language, and social practices. Discourse is what gets to be said, who gets to say it, with what authority, and with what effects.
3  For more on social constructs and social construction, see Searle (1995) and Gergen (2009).
4  This is an important distinction between social *constructivism* and social *construction*. Unfortunately, much of the literature confuses the two and uses them interchangeably. Social constructivism actually *emphasizes* the "in the head" process that individuals use to make meaning of their own ostensibly individual perceptions. In contrast, social construction concerns itself with the meanings people negotiate *together* in the social world.
5  It's worth reading more on this from Foucault (1965, 1973, 1977). He contends that the invention of the individual has led to practices of objectification and subjugation through "dividing practices" and "scientific classification." Also, Sampson (2008) asserts that the self-contained individual exists in order to maintain modern power. He maintains that North American psychology's allegiance to the self-contained individual is not evidence of the idea's validity as a "natural" fact; rather, psychology's focus on the self-contained individual simply serves to uphold the social structure.
6  Foucault writes of *dividing practices*, *scientific classification*, and *subjectification* as ways in which power operates to make people into objects for study and control. Subjectification is especially relevant here because it emphasizes the ways in which people participate in self-formation or identification.
7  When I'm in relationship with any particular young person, I always ask myself, *Who do I need to be?* or, perhaps more accurately, *In what way can I show up so that this person can be their best self?* We make each other.
8  Gay-Straight Alliance (GSA) groups provide social support and activities for students in many schools.
9  Here, *resistant* means to stand against the limits and regulations of the prevailing discourse. This meaning is similar to *acts of resistance* in an activist context. This use of the term honors and respects the construction of alternative identities.
10  Text is anything that produces meaning. This includes language, images, memes, concepts, etc.

# 2

# POWER TO THE PEOPLE

## Positioning and Author-ity

As you enter positions of trust and power, dream a little before you think.

*Toni Morrison*[1]

I want to approach youth from a framework of possibility, to ask them, "What could be possible?"

*Emily, a youth worker*

Chapter 1 laid out the basics of social construction, giving you a philosophical place where you can anchor your practice. This will be the place that you're coming from—the place that provides you with a perspective on the world and on people in relationship.

All of this was big picture stuff, and you're probably more than ready to dig into what this looks like in your daily interactions with youth. But before we jump into those specific skills, there are a few more concepts that you need to become familiar with.

## Choosing Your Lane: Positioning

I often stop myself when I'm talking out loud. I stop myself from having an idea and I check with them: "Do you want me to listen or lay it out?"

*Val, a youth worker*

How does social construction influence the way we show up to youth work? When we understand that language is productive and identities are relational, what else does this mean in terms of the flesh-and-blood young people we're interacting with?

One key influence involves *positioning* (Harre & Van Langenhove, 1999). Positioning has to do with the way you situate yourself in relationship to young people. It also has to do with how you're situated in relation to the discourses that influence your identity, each youth's identity, and your relationship with them. Taking note of how you're positioned is a critical aspect of accounting for the power and authority you have in young people's lives. This authority comes from being positioned culturally as an adult and professionally as a youth worker. Accounting for this authority means, in part, choosing a relational stance that positions young people as competent agents who can speak with authority about their lives (Tilsen, 2013).

For example, you can choose to position yourself in a way that creates space for a young person to make decisions and exercise agency in their life. This doesn't mean that you are inconsequential to the interaction; it means that you decenter (but not dismiss) yourself within the conversation and position yourself in collaboration with the young person. At other times, you may choose to position yourself in ways that center the authority you carry.

Positioning has to do with how you define yourself *in this particular relationship, at this particular time, for the purpose at hand.* Are you, for example, positioning yourself as expert or as not-knowing, as authority or as collaborator, as in control or in partnership? There isn't a one-size-fits-all-situations position that you can take.

Positioning is about taking up a relational identity that encourages all the participants to show up and be their best selves. In other words, you want to position yourself so that (1) the conversation is as meaningful as possible to the young person you're engaging with, and (2) they get positioned in a way that is most meaningful and productive for them.

That second point is critical: *when we position ourselves, we also position our conversational partner(s).* Suppose that I show up in class, stand behind the lectern, read from my notes and slides, never invite questions or comments, and never seek student input. I have not only taken a position as a boring and authoritative pedagogue, but I have positioned my students as bored and unimportant to the learning process. Alternatively, suppose that my class sits in a circle that I'm a part of, I bring snacks, there's coffee and tea available, I welcome comments, and I encourage my students to discuss and challenge the course material in class. Then I have positioned myself in a way that positions my students in a particular way as well.

Similarly, if you dictate the content of a conversation, center your ideas rather than those of the young person, and prevent them from asking questions and influencing the conversation, you're making positioning decisions for both of you. That may make sense if you are directing the youth through a dangerous situation. But it may not be the best way to position yourself if you are, for example, meeting to explore their interest in joining a theater group.

The best way to position yourself depends on the context and purpose of the interaction, and on what is going on in that moment.

---

**#FergusonSyllabus Question**

How do you position yourself to join youth in acts of resistance to unjust systems of power?

Think about what it means to do something with someone. Now think about what it means to do something to someone. What are the differences? What might each of these positions look like? Consider the effects of misogyny, racism, cissexism, classism, homophobia, and other systems of oppression that impact young people. How do these factors influence your decisions about positioning?

---

## Centeredness and Influence

I check myself if I notice I'm more excited than they are.

*Val, a youth worker*

Michael White (2007) identified two aspects of positioning that I have adapted for youth workers: *centeredness* and *influence*.

White was concerned about the history of "expert" knowledge being overly centered in relationships with people who seek therapeutic services. He did not want to continue a tradition of erasing people's own skills and knowledges by imposing professional ideas on them. As youth workers, we can relate to this concern: we do not want to have adult ideas overshadowing those of young people. White also recognized, however, that professionals have skills that they bring to their encounters with others and that these need to be acknowledged. Indeed, that is why people seek out professionals. Young people involved with youth workers expect to get something from their interactions.

White suggested that we take a stance of being *decentered and influential* with those who seek our help. A *decentered* position ensures that the youth worker relationally steps aside to position the young person in the center of the conversation. Being *influential* acknowledges that the youth worker has an impact through what they bring to the relationship and through their facilitative role as a conversationalist.

Being *centered* means that one's ideas, stories, and agenda are the foci of the interaction. To the extent that one is centered, the interaction privileges *that person's* knowledges and influence on the conversation. Being *decentered* means that one's ideas, meanings, and knowledges do not make up the "stuff" of the conversation. But note that being decentered does not mean being unengaged or uninfluential.

Furthermore, centeredness is not a set of binary options; that is, if one person is centered, that does not render the other completely decentered. Rather, the degree of centeredness is flexible, fluid, and responsive to the people involved and the situation at hand.

Being *influential*, the second aspect of White's stance, means that one has an impact, a say in what happens in the conversational moment. This might involve what gets to be talked about, how it's talked about, who's talking, and what direction the talking is headed in. *Being influential with a young person invites their centeredness.* When a youth worker positions themselves as decentered and influential, they use their skills to facilitate a conversation or experience that centers a young person's own preferences, ideas, and knowledges.

Influence, like centeredness, is not binary. In any relationship or interaction, the degree of influence varies in response to the people involved and the circumstances they're in. Furthermore, influence can be understood as mutual; both members of a conversation can influence the interaction—and thus, each other. In this way, positioning naturally becomes relational.

It's helpful to ask yourself certain questions about the effects of your own centeredness and influence. For example:

- What happens with any particular young person when I am more centered? Less centered? More influential? Less influential? In each case, what becomes possible, and what gets shut down?
- In what circumstances does *decreasing* my influence position youth in ways that help them? Exactly how does this help them?
- In what circumstances does *increasing* my influence position them in ways that help them? Exactly how does this help them?
- What contextual and personal factors might affect my positioning? How can I be aware of and account for these?

When we consider centeredness and influence as flexible, relationally responsive dimensions of positioning, we free ourselves from the rigidity of showing up in a one-size-fits-all way. Please note that centeredness and influence are not things you decide on in advance, or even in the moment, and then simply maintain. They involve continuous reflection and, often, adjustment.

How you're positioned with youth has significant implications about power relations. When you're intentional about how you position yourself with youth, you reject all assumptions about what relationships between adults and youth, or professionals and youth, *should be*. You avoid reproducing and participating in power relations that privilege adults and professionals while marginalizing young people. This creates space for a reworking of power relations. This can generate many new and significant identities for both young people and you.

---

### Positioning When You Need to Show Up with Authority

Positioning is determined in part by the purpose of your interaction and the situation at hand. Sometimes, you may need to situate yourself in ways that emphasize and leverage the formal authority you have in your professional position. For example, you may need to be very directive when someone is injured or if there is some other emergency. Also, you may need to assert your authority when addressing young people about actions that they need to be accountable for.

The challenge when taking a stance of authority is *to do so in a way that maintains the dignity of the young person*. This is possible even if you are not able to take the time to listen to their preferences or ask questions (as would often be the case in an emergency), or if you have to make rapid decisions about consequences for someone's actions. For example, with emergencies you can often meet and listen to a young person after the crisis is addressed.

When dealing with difficult situations, it helps to be transparent, to use externalizing language (which I'll discuss in Chapter 8), and to be clear that your relationship with the young person is not in jeopardy. These are all ways to honor the dignity of the person, while inviting and encouraging them to take responsibility.

---

## Power Up, Down, and All Around

> Where there is power, there is resistance.
>
> *Michel Foucault*

> I asked him if I could talk to him. I told him it's his option, we don't have to talk. Then he stood up and we walked out together to talk.
>
> *Jenna D., a youth worker*

Now let's consider the relationship of positioning to power. The ideas of Michel Foucault (1978, 2000) inform how power is conceptualized in social construction and post-structural theory.[2] An essential feature of Foucault's analysis of power is that power is everywhere. We are all always participating in power relations.

Power is about exerting influence. This influence occurs not only on a large social or cultural scale; it is a regular aspect of all our interactions. Furthermore, power is not necessarily bad or good. It is always operating, in multiple directions. And power is relational and contextual.

Unlike in liberal humanist and structural accounts of power, from a social constructionist view, power is not a commodity that certain people have and others do not, based on their abilities and the choices they make (liberal humanism), or their social location and place in society (structural). From a post-structural perspective, it is literally impossible for there to be relations among people where power is not involved (Monk, Winslade, & Sinclair, 2008).

For instance, you'll recall my earlier example in which I described teaching in an oppressive and authoritarian way. This could be described as an act of power: teaching in a rigid, controlling manner that does not allow for students to approach me and influence the class. However, if some of the students spent the class drawing, or listening to music through their ear buds, or messaging each other about how awful I am, those would be acts of resistance—power in response to power (Foucault, 1978). Although these acts may not change the students' condition of being in a boring classroom with an exhausting instructor, those acts of resistance would still matter, because they say something about students' greater intentions for themselves and their desire to be more than depositories of boring lecture notes.

This is an example of Foucault's assertion that *power is productive*. That is, power is about people taking action or speaking out in order to produce themselves in particular ways. Thus, while my positioning and pedagogy may have been an effort to produce obedient, sycophant students, the students engaged in acts of resistance to produce themselves as people who refused to assume that obedient status.

Now let's imagine that, after my class is over, my students get together and tell each other stories of what they did to resist. In doing this, they engage in discursive production: circulating stories that produce themselves as active agents rather than passive receptacles.

## Language and Power

> "Choice" is a dilemma for urban Native youth; they can't choose if they're not de-colonized from dominant discourses.
>
> *Angela, a youth worker*

Like power, language is productive. This means that language constructs the worlds we live in, that it has real effects. Some of these are positive, some negative—though of course this always depends on one's position and perspective.

We have already seen that discourse plays a defining role in how power flows through society and in how identities are constructed. Indeed, Burr (2003) observes that "language is the crucible of change, both personal and social" (p. 56). I am not merely talking about "powerful words," or "strong talk," or "harsh language." I am talking about the power to construct and regulate narratives that put forth notions of what is and isn't acceptable.

Remember, discourse is defined as *what gets to be said, by whom, with what authority, and with what effects*. Because particular discourses have particular effects on certain people—and because we can't avoid engaging in practices of power (since power is always operating in all relationships)—an ethical question arises: what practices of power should we engage in (Monk, Winslade, & Sinclair, 2008)? Which ones should we avoid or disrupt?

We have already briefly examined the skepticism that social construction holds toward truth claims. When we question taken-for-granted assumptions about what we know and how we know it, we are interrogating power. Both this skepticism and this interrogation are acts of resistance—another form of power.

Consider this example: Lea is a 19-year-old woman who lives with her two-year-old daughter Alexis in a transitional housing program for young moms. In addition to 24-hour building supervision, youth workers provide supportive case management and advocacy for the young residents. They also structure groups, activities, and community experiences on topics that interest the young moms.

When Lea first joins the program, she talks with the other participants and the staff about how she sees herself as a slut and a loser. She explains to some of them that she is "damaged goods that no one will want," and she struggles to articulate ways in which she is "worth anything" outside of "being someone's woman." She had been certain that her baby's father was in love with her and that they would "be a family together." She was devastated when he disappeared from her life a week before she delivered their daughter. From a narrative perspective, Lea was contending with a *totalizing description* of her identity—i.e. one founded on a singular account or story (in Lea's case, being a slut, damaged goods, etc.), at the expense of all other stories, aspects, and identities in one's life.

Through conversations with youth workers and group discussions that included her peers, Lea was encouraged to question things that she had always held to be unshakable truths—things that upheld this totalizing story. In a group activity, her peers identified some of the assumptions that the discourse of slut shaming is based on. Then they came up with questions about that discourse to expose the assumptions held within it. Here are some of those assumptions followed by questions:

- *Assumption: Women are sluts, but men aren't.* What is it that makes you a slut? If your boyfriend had stayed with you, would you still be a slut? If women are called sluts but men aren't, and both men and women like to have sex, what does that say about women and their enjoyment of sex?
- *Assumption: Everyone thinks I'm a slut.* Who has called you a slut? Who hasn't called you a slut? What are your relationships like with each of these groups of people?
- *Assumption: It's okay to call someone a slut if they are one.* Have you ever called anyone a slut? Why or why not? What made you think or say that about someone? How did you feel when you called someone that? Who decides who qualifies to be a slut?

- *Assumption*: *Being a slut nullifies everything else about you.* Do you think that being a slut makes someone less valuable or capable as a person? If someone is a slut, does that cancel out everything else about them?
- *Assumption*: *Sex is okay for men, but not for women.* If women and girls become sluts when they have sex, how come men and boys don't become sluts when they have sex? Is sex only for men? If so, shouldn't they be having sex only with each other?
- *Assumption*: *Certain qualities or actions make someone a slut.* What is the opposite of a slut? What are the requirements to not be a slut? Are these requirements the same for everyone?
- *Assumption*: *Heterosexual sex is the norm.* Can queer women be sluts? Why or why not? How are queer female sluts different from, or the same as, straight female sluts?
- *Assumption*: *Whether or not women are considered sluts is based on their relationship with men.* Does it seem right that what your boyfriend does determines whether or not you're considered a slut?
- *Assumption*: *Men's identity is not based on their relationship with women.* If you had left him, would he be a slut? Why not?
- *Assumption*: *The rules are different for men than for women.* Why are they different, and in what ways? Who makes up these rules? Who benefits from those rules? Who suffers because of them?
- *Assumption*: *Sex is only right within a forever relationship.* Where does the idea that you're supposed to have one sexual partner forever come from? What ideas from the media, pop culture, religion, or your family got you to believe this? Does this mean that everyone who's ever had sex with someone other than their forever partner is a slut?

These questions, created by this group of young women, helped Lea see that the discourse of slut shaming is made possible by a set of assumptions that, upon scrutiny, reflect oppressive standards of sexual conduct. These standards support other unjust discourses as well, such as patriarchy, misogyny, sex negativity, and heteronormativity. Once these assumptions were loosened up, Lea and her peers were able to consider rejecting the slut-shaming discourse as one that did not account for who they are and who they hoped to become. This discourse had neither the complete nor the final say in who they were, what they could be, and what they could do in the world.

In addition, these young women were able to give new and preferred meanings to their experiences as sexually active young women. They replaced the slut-shaming discourses with discourses of sex positivity,[3] self-reliance, and feminism. By questioning the taken-for-granted status of the slut-shaming discourse, the young moms made way for the discursive production of new identities located within these counter discourses. They replaced a totalizing description with a variety of stories that reflected the complexities of their identities and that honored the multiple contexts in which they lived.

## Gaining Author-ity

> Youth of color know they're colonized; I help them find the language to express that.
>
> *Marjaan, a youth worker*

So far, we've discussed (1) an awareness of our positioning and power relations as an act of accountability, and (2) the ways in which power operates through language. Understanding these considerations helps us as youth workers to support young people in assuming *author-ity* over their own stories. *Author-ity* is a mnemonic I use to highlight the productive power located in the ability to write, speak, and live one's own experience from one's own perspective.

Earlier, I noted that social construction holds that we are not the only authors of our stories. This is because our individual stories gain meaning through the cultural stories—or discourses—that are available to us. Understanding positioning and how language operates allows us to support youth in their personal meaning making within these discourses.

Some discourses have marginalizing effects on the author-ity of young people. Most notably, ageist and adultist discourses diminish youth knowledge, agency, and author-ity. These discourses are commonly embodied in phrases such as *You'll understand when you're older*; *You're too young to decide*; and *He's only (fill in an age)*. In addition, any discourse that imposes specifications of normality or normal behavior can override youth "story telling rights" (Denborough, 2014). Lastly, when a young person experiences a problem, the discourses that support the problem can often take the pen out of their hands and—as we saw with Lea—write a totalizing account that denies them all author-ity.

Gaining personal story telling rights within influential discourses involves identifying or constructing *counter discourses*—discourses that stand in resistance to prevailing discourses and that also give meaning to a young person's preferred stories. As we saw with Lea and the other young moms, counter discourses become available when we move from totalizing descriptions to multiple and complex stories that invite alternative meanings generated from experience. By exercising author-ity, young people become active participants in their identity construction, rather than passive recipients of societal labels and the limiting stories that they carry.

Understanding the links between social construction, positioning theory, and discourse provides a critical foundation for your youth work practice. This understanding respects youths' agency to imagine and construct identities that stand against problematic (and, often, prevailing) discourses.

When we understand that (and how) language is productive, we can question narratives that have been constructed in ways that tell a single story. These totalizing accounts pigeonhole youth, at the expense of other stories that offer richer and more contextual understandings of their experiences. When these totalizing accounts are questioned, counter discourses and the stories they generate can emerge from the margins to challenge them.

## Summary

Power *does* something: it exerts influence over others. It is not inherently good or bad; it all depends on what its effects are and who is evaluating them.

Youth work done from a constructionist stance accounts for the effects of power. One way we attempt this is through intentional positioning: how we situate ourselves with others, and within the various contexts that we work. When we position ourselves, we also implicitly position the other people we're engaging with. Decisions about positioning depend on how others respond and what the purpose of our engagement is. A life-or-death emergency on a wilderness adventure would require that we position ourselves very differently than a conversation over coffee with several young people who are planning the wilderness trip.

We also need to attend to the ways power operates through language. We are interested in the effects of discourses on young people's ability to exercise author-ity over their personal stories. We can work with youth to expose the assumptions embedded within discourses that produce totalizing descriptions at the expense of more complex accounts of youth identity.

## Highlights

### *Liberal-Humanism vs. Structural vs. Post-Structural*

The chart below compares a post-structural analysis of power to those of liberal-humanism and structuralism.[4]

| | *Liberal-Humanism* | *Structural* | *Post-Structural* |
|---|---|---|---|
| Locates Power in... | The individual (essentialism) | Systems/social locations | Discourse |
| Power Is... | A limited commodity based on an individual's essential skills | A limited commodity based on group membership | Inherent to social relations, and something we are always participating in |
| Access to Power | We are all born equal/personal choices/ meritocracy | We are born into social locations/ dismantle or change power structure | Through social practices, discursive production, and resistance |
| Key Metaphor | Personal power | Systemic/institutional power | Discursive power |
| Goal of Analysis | Elevating the individual | Structural change | Deconstruction; resistance to hegemony |

## Key Terms

1. **Author-ity:** A mnemonic used to highlight the productive power located in the ability to write, speak, and live one's own experience from one's own perspective.
2. **Counter discourse:** A discourse that stands in contrast to any dominant discourse, particularly one that writes problematic and/or totalizing stories. Counter discourses support alternative preferred stories.
3. **Decentered and influential:** This stance centers youths' knowledge, not your own, while you remain influential in the relationship and the process. This is in contrast to being centered (in which *your* knowledge and preferences as a youth worker are privileged) and to being non-influential (in which you have no impact on the process or the relationship).
4. **Positioning:** How you situate yourself in relationship to the young people you work with, and the discourses that influence that work. Position is also called **stance** or **posture**. Positioning is based on how power operates in our relationships.
5. **Power:** Anything that does something and has effects. Power is not inherently good or bad; any evaluation of power needs to be based on what it does, whom it benefits or hurts, etc.
6. **Resistance:** Standing up to, or acting against, any form of power that has limiting, specifying, or marginalizing effects. Resistance is important because it reflects what matters to people and because it is an expression ᵒᶠ power responding to power.
7. **Story telling rights:** Story telling rights (Denbo to the idea of author-ity: they specify who has shape, name, and tell a story.
8. **Totalizing:** A totalizing description or account of identity is based on a single story from one perspective, leaving out all other perspectives or dimensions of identity.

## Discussion Questions

1. What would be your preferred positioning with a young person when you're meeting them for the first time? Why?
2. What position might be the most challenging for you (for example, collaborator, authority, expert)? Why?
3. How have you typically understood power? What about that understanding makes sense to you? What does not?
4. What have been some totalizing descriptions others have made about you? What were the effects of these on you? On your relationship with the people who accepted or used those totalizing descriptions?

## Notes

1 Commencement speech at City College, quoted in: (No byline). (1988, May 28). Commencement. *New York Times.*
2 There are two other major analyses of power that have great influence on Western culture: the liberal-humanist view and the structural perspective. Both of these are reflected in many of the assumptions we have about people's relationship with power. A chart comparing these three perspectives appears at the end of this chapter.
3 Sex positivity rejects a moralizing posture in favor of an attitude that honors consensual sexual activities, recognizes and celebrates sexual diversity, and emphasizes sexual pleasure rather than danger and sin.
4 See Monk, Winslade, and Sinclair (2008) for a thorough account and comparison of these three frameworks of power.

# 3

# RESPONSE-ABILITY

## Relational Ethics and an Ethic of Care

It is clear that ethics cannot be formulated.

Ludwig Wittgenstein, *Tractatus
Logico-Philosophicus*

Loving the young people we work with—that's part of my ethics.

*Quinn, a youth worker*

As we saw in the previous chapters, constructionist-informed youth work is very interested in power relations, the generative properties of language, and the meanings people make together in relationship. This focus on power, language, and relational meaning making both influences and reflects an orientation of *relational ethics*. This chapter looks closely at relational ethics and how they support a youth work practice based on accountability to, and justice for, young people.

## Ethics Are More Than We Think

Exposing the oppressive systems that impact youths' lives is central to my ethics.

*Mickella, a youth worker*

Let's try a little free association. When you hear "ethics," what's the very next word that comes to mind?

If you said *dilemma, conflict, or problem*, you're not alone. Or maybe you thought about legal issues and policies, or avoiding problems. When I ask students and youth workers about their own relationship with ethics, their responses usually fall into this set of terms. Often, they just groan.

---

**Ethics and You**

How would you describe your relationship with youth work ethics?

What has shaped or influenced the relationship you have with these ethics?

What does it mean to say that someone's youth work practice is ethical? How do you know that this is what it means?

What does it mean to say that someone's youth work practice is *not* ethical? How do you know that this is what it means?

---

The less-than-warm feelings many youth workers have about ethics likely come from the way ethics have become disembodied from the whole of youth work practice.[1] We typically turn to them only when there's a dilemma or a problem. Indeed, because *ethics* has, more and more, come to mean legal issues and avoiding problems, fear and risk aversion often accompany any discussion of the subject. After we consult agency rules, local laws, and professional codes (if any exist for youth work in our jurisdiction) to deal with some issue that's in our face, we return to our regularly scheduled work. Then ethics take a back seat until something else ominous comes up. In short, ethics have come to be about following and applying (usually in a one size fits all way) the specified, codified rules that have been created miles away from the conversational moment.

Surely, we can do better than this. Jennifer White (2011) calls for "an enlarged view of ethics" in relationship-based practices (p. 44). *Relational ethics* (McNamee, 2009, 2015) offer youth workers the kind of expanded, generative version of ethics that White envisions. This approach to ethics focuses attention on the *process of being in a relationship*, rather than on isolated actions (such as ethical "dilemmas").

Ethics, like power, are part of and central to everything we do. This is one of the distinguishing features of relational ethics: they are expanded beyond the realm of risk management and problem avoidance, and placed in the heart of practice. Reynolds (2012, 2014) calls this practice *centering ethics*.

In most conventional approaches to youth work, we organize our work around goals (e.g. positive youth development) and techniques (e.g. motivational interviewing); meanwhile, ethics become an ancillary consideration. When we do this, our ethical framework is not always visible.

According to Reynolds, however, when we center our ethics we move toward one of social construction's most pragmatic and important intentions. We privilege *the effects of what we do*, rather than our ability to "properly" apply a technique. Indeed, sometimes we can be technically proficient, but relationally deficient because there is no universal "right" way to engage with all youth. This is a central tenet of social construction: avoid universality, focus instead on relational responsiveness and engagement. Centering relational ethics helps us live into our values and intentions of centering the relationship.

Relational ethics are essential to any practice informed by social construction. When we practice from a constructionist stance, ethics are the blood that courses through the body of our work. We orient our work toward *relational responsibility* (McNamee & Gergen, 1999). I think of this as *relational response-ability*—that is, building the skills and capacity necessary for responding to the needs of relationships.

An important aspect of relational response-ability is an *ethic of care*. In the 1980s, feminist scholars (e.g. Gilligan, 1982; Noddings, 1984) sought ways to understand ethics and morality that reflected the lived experiences of women. This led to the articulation of an ethic of care. Such an ethic rejects universal ideas of moral development and instead focuses on the needs of specific people and specific relationships. In this context, *care* is not only a response to suffering; it is an essential component of all relationships at all times.

Practices of caring involve attending and responding to people's needs, looking after their best interests, and promoting the well-being and potential of people and their relationships. In youth work, this means that care is emphasized within each relationship we have with each young person. Each relationship becomes a place of caring.

Let's take a closer look at relational ethics and what they look like in youth work practice.

## Power and Positioning as Ethical Acts

How I show up has a huge influence on how youth show up.

*Jena B., a youth worker*

Ethics are about how power operates and how it affects people. As we've seen, power is always operating in relationships. Thus, everything we do—or don't do—in relationships has ethical implications. We've also seen how power operates through discourse and social practices. Consequently, our decisions about positioning and the discourses we engage in are ethical acts.

What does this look like in youth work practice? Consider this example from Jamal, a youth worker in a summer parks program whom I consulted with:

Jamal voiced his frustration with a group of fourth and fifth graders. He described spending a lot of time carefully planning arts and crafts projects, playground games, community outings, and creative writing and theater activities. Jamal explained that he is "super organized—I come ready with a plan every day." Despite having things, in Jamal's words, "planned to a T," the youth "don't take it seriously, and they test me all the time."

I asked Jamal what he meant by "they test me." Jamal said, "You know, pushing back and seeing if I'll stick to my plan, or if they can make me change." As we talked further, Jamal explained that his intentions are "to be consistent and fair with them." He also said that if he were to change things in response to pressure from young people, he would be betraying these values. He added, "I get that kids test adults; they need to see where the boundaries are."

Let's take a closer look at what Jamal said. By understanding young people as "testing" him, Jamal chose the particular discourse of *behavior*, a very dominant idea in our culture. His positioning as an authority in charge fits this frame. He also articulated an ethic of consistency and fairness, common components of a behavioral framework.[2]

In considering the ethics of this situation, it isn't a matter of finding the *correct* ethical approach. Instead, we can ask, *What are the effects of Jamal's choices of discourse and positioning?*

One effect was the frustration that Jamal felt. Often, when we experience frustration in our work with young people, it's because we are unable to practice in ways that allow us to live into our ethics. Frustration is one common response to the constraints that keep us from putting into practice the ethics that inspire us. Other effects of the discourse and positioning that Jamal chose were the response of the young people, and, in turn, Jamal's response to them. According to Jamal, he spent less time in activities than he would like and more time trying to enforce his plans. He also acknowledged that his relationships with the youth had suffered. Sighing, he told me, "None of us is having the kind of fun we thought we'd have in this program."

During this consultation, Jamal articulated an ethic of "respecting youth and meeting them where they're at." We explored what this meant to him and considered whether taking a "hard line on keeping plans" reflected these values. We explored questions such as: *What alternative positions would better reflect your ethics—and, perhaps, receive a more positive response? What understanding of power would help you create better connections with the young people?* These are ethical questions, not merely technical ones.

As Jamal and I discussed his ideas about respecting youth, he shifted his understanding of the young people's actions in response to his plans from *testing* to *protesting*. Here is an excerpt from our consultation:

JULIE: When you were first thinking that the group was "testing" you, how did that impact your ability to show up in your ethic of meeting them where they're at?

JAMAL: Yeah, that's just it. I'm realizing now that the more I doubled down on that idea, the further I got from listening to the youth and what mattered to them. I think that this idea that kids test adults is really strong, like, something we hear all the time. Hell, I heard that from my mom and teachers all the time! Sure, sometimes youth *are* testing if you mean what you say you're gonna do, but when you think about youth as *testers*—like that's who they *are*—it really takes you away from what you believe and how you want to do youth work.

JULIE: Is there a way that sorting out the difference between "testing" and "testers" is helping you think about ways to meet the group where they're at?

JAMAL: Yeah, well, it's something they're doing, not who they are, so I think I'm seeing more about who they are.

JULIE: How does that help you do the things you want to do and be the youth worker you want to be in relationship to them?

JAMAL: If I don't see them as testers, I don't have to be whoever it is that maintains whatever they're testing. In this case, it's my plans! Sticking to my plans kept me from sticking to my values.

JULIE: Cool. Sounds like you're seeing the relationship between how you show up and how the kids show up, is that right?

JAMAL: Totally.

JULIE: Okay, if they're not testing and they're not testers, what are they doing and who can you see them as that positions you in a way to stick with your values?

JAMAL: I think they're protesting my dumb-ass plans and stubbornness! They're protesters!

JULIE: You can get behind a protest and protesters?

JAMAL: Oh, hell, yeah! That's why I do youth work! I want to see young people organizing and protesting in ways that allow them to influence their own lives. I just didn't think I'd be the one they'd have to stand up to!

JULIE: Pretty awesome for them that it is you, someone who honors youth and protesters!

This conversation opened space for an alternative discourse that centered on youth agency and liberation—values that fit Jamal's ethics. This allowed him to assume the position of ally, which in turn opened him up to hearing the young people's feedback about his planning. Then, and only then, was he able to make room for them to contribute to the group activities. For Jamal, taking youth seriously, responding to their concerns, and integrating their feedback into programming ultimately embodied his ethics.

Jamal's situation serves as an important example of how we youth workers—despite our stated ethics, intentions, and analysis of power operations—can experience what I call *ethics drift*. We can unwittingly stray from our values and intentions—often partly because of the pressures of prevailing cultural practices. This is why centering our ethics and developing practices that reflect them is crucial.

Centering ethics and attending to power requires each of us to ask ourselves: *Does my practice reveal something other than my stated intentions and ethics?* Said another way, *Is what I intend to do in my work apparent in what I actually do?*

You will be hard-pressed to find a youth worker who says that they want to be unethical and unhelpful in their work with youth. People typically have good intentions. Yet they do not always practice them. In the example before, Jamal was frustrated, in part, because he got caught up in a prevailing idea about how adults are supposed to respond to young people. It is easy to be influenced by the pressures of competing discourses, especially those that specify how to be an adult or a professional with young people. Making a shift to relationally engaged youth work will help you stand in your own ethics.

---

### #FergusonSyllabus Question

Can we do ethical youth work without considering systemic factors of oppression?

Is it ethical to engage young people in fun and interesting experiences and conversations, to facilitate opportunities and offer resources, and to do other youth work activities with them as individuals, without doing anything to transform (or help them transform) the racist/sexist/homophobic/classist culture they live in?

---

## From Rules to Relationships: Facilitating the Shift

> Sitting in front of an authority figure can feel hostile. Even when a youth got kicked out of class, I'd go for a walk with them to disrupt that power dynamic and make a connection.
>
> *Sam, a youth worker*

A constructionist stance requires a shift from one culture of practice to another. We move ethics from an ancillary function reserved for challenging situations to a central place informing all practice. Here are some specific aspects of this shift:

1.  **Shifting from a culture of one size fits all rules to a culture of relational engagement.** Conventional ethical practices follow a one-size-fits-all approach. Rules are established and guidelines are set that are intended to be applied universally. As we've seen, the rejection of universality is a core tenet of social construction. In fact, from a constructionist perspective, it is inherently *unethical* to apply the same ideas of right and wrong to all people in all contexts. There is simply too great a diversity of worldviews, and too many unique situations, to believe that a single static

moral framework (especially one produced by the dominant group, such as a professional code of conduct) can be effective and respectful for all people in all situations.

Ethics as flexible and fluid is not a theoretical abstraction or ideal. It means being attuned and responsive to the people and contexts in which we work. At its core, youth work is about challenging grand narratives that impose "truths" on young people that dictate and limit how they can show up in the world.

2. **Shifting from a culture that privileges professional knowledges and ethical codes to one that centers youth and their local knowledges.** The move fr  niversal truths t multiple contexts means that professional kno                              privilege or status over those of the people we work with. This also means that professional ideas and practices, as well as ethical codes, are considered alongside the values and worldviews of the youth and communities we work with. While not all of these may not be formalized as codes of ethics, every community and culture has a moral order, an understanding of what is right and wrong based on the meanings made within the relational sphere of that community. From an ethic of relational responsibility (McNamee & Gergen, 1999), it is incumbent on us to be open to and curious about the worlds of other people and what matters to them.

3. **Shifting from a culture of imposing ethics to a way of doing ethics in a relationship.** When we eschew universality and decenter professional knowledges and practices, we no longer have the imagined certainty that we are promised by the specific practices of codified guidelines. Thus, the imposition of professional knowledges and codes gets replaced by collaboration and relational and cultural responsiveness. *Doing* rather than *imposing* ethics becomes a shared process of negotiating and making meaning. This includes evaluating the effects of particular actions and non-actions, and guarding against the injustice of colonizing others into our worldview.

4. **Shifting from a culture of codes of conduct to a relational stance.** Ultimately, relational ethics is about creating ethical practice from the inside out, rather than the outside in. That is, conventional ethics are informed by a universal code that is imposed from the outside—and that is produced far from the interactional moment, the cultural context, and the relationship of the youth worker and the particular young person. In contrast, relational ethics is a matter of positioning. It's about your stance in relation to your profession, the community you work in, the young people you work with, and your own intentions. Relational responsibility happens *from inside* each unique relationship. It responds to and honors the local values of the communities you serve.

*(Adapted from McNamee, 2009)*

## Ethics as Questions

> We always have to ask what are we doing and what are the effects on youth.
>
> *Emily, a youth worker*

Another way to facilitate the shift from rules to relationships is to consider *ethics as questions*. Typically, we think about *ethical questions*: specific dilemmas or complicated situations that present u          illenges. These are not what I'm discussing here. I'm talking abou         ) approach and encounter ethics.

Rather than having specific ethical codes as gι          Freedman and Combs (1996) offer *ethics expressed as questions*. These          ; are consistent with the ideas of centering ethics, an ethic of care,          onal response-ability, because they focus on our relationships with          )ple and invite us to reflect on our practice and its effects. We reflect          ns that help us examine our assumptions about young people, youth          ι relationships; about the practice of youth work; and about the effec          ρractice. Some examples of ethics as questions include:

- How does this model or theory explain young people?
- How does it expect you to act in your work?
- How does it expect young people to act with you?
- How would you describe the positioning encouraged by this practice?
- Who is considered to have knowledge and expertise?
- Who enters whose world?
- Does this way of doing youth work foster normativity or generativity? How?
- What are the effects of this practice on youth? On their relationships with important other people in their lives? On the communities they belong to?
- What is valued in this model or theory? What is devalued or disvalued?

*(Adapted from Freedman and Combs, 1996)*

Through the deliberate consideration of questions about what we do and what effects our actions have, we become actively accountable to the youth we work with. Being *accountable to* rather than *accountable for* young people further reflects the shift to an ethic of care and relational response-ability. This shift removes the paternalistic implication often embedded within conventional ethics, while remaining attentive to the power relations inherent in adult-youth relationships.

The common arguments against relational ethics are (1) that it promotes relativism and (2) that it renders all stories and constructions as equally valid. According to this argument, while a universalizing ethics ignores complexity, a relativizing ethics leads to an "anything goes" attitude in which a moral argument could be made for abuse, violence, or some other egregious act.

Yet that is not at all what relational ethics is about. When we shift our focus from isolated acts to interactive processes, we acknowledge that all actions make sense in context, and we question who has the authority to decide what the definitive context will be (McNamee, 2015). Thus, our ethical inquiry focuses on exploring power relations.[3] This creates space for cultures, perspectives, and discourses other than those that inform professional codes and the norms of mainstream adult society. This is especially important for youth, and even more so for young people who come from marginalized or oppressed communities.

This *doesn't* mean that we treat all stories equally or that everything is "just relative." It *does* mean, however, that we examine our practices from multiple perspectives instead of only from the dominant discourse that informs professional youth work. Freedman and Combs (1996) call this a *margin-in* approach to ethics: the experience of those who live on the margins of dominant society and who experience systemic oppression are valued and considered. Rather than evaluating ethics on the extent to which particular rules are followed, we evaluate them on the effects of what we do.

As you read the vignette that follows, ask yourself whether or not the youth worker acted ethically in this situation.

Mycah works at an agency that provides services for youth, including advocacy and resource assistance, case management, meals, basic supplies, and a drop-in space with games, computers, and washers and dryers The center is located in a busy downtown neighborhood of a large city.

Mycah is in her office, conversing with a young man she's known for a while. After a few minutes, he gets up and says, "Sorry for being so fidgety. It's really uncomfortable to sit." Before Mycah can ask him what's wrong, he pulls a gun out of his pants and apologizes. "I'm really sorry I brought this in here today. I needed it for a possible situation earlier, and I didn't have a chance to stash it. I would've been late to our meeting if I ditched it first."

He sets it on the side table. Mycah asks if it's loaded, and he reaches into his book bag to show her the bullets. "Nah, I took them out real quick. I didn't want to scare you if I had to rearrange things."

After talking for a while, she asks him where he's headed and how he's getting there. "I'm headed to the shelter to meet with my case manager. I got tokens—I'll take the bus."

Mycah is concerned about him taking the bus. He has had some run-ins with the transit cops, and they have been increasing their surveillance of youth on public transit. Mycah decides to give him a ride back to the shelter in her car.

What do you think—did Mycah act ethically or not? Why or why not? Does Mycah's response point to an "anything goes" relativism? Or does it reflect her consideration of the multiple perspectives involved and the possible effects of her actions (or inaction)? Also consider the following questions:

- What assumptions and beliefs about ethical practice does your position reflect?
- What is being valued in your position? What is not being valued?

- What are other ways of understanding this situation?
- Can you identify the different perspectives and relationships involved in this story? What are the ethical concerns within each perspective? What is being valued in each of them?

Depending on your own work, Mycah's situation may seem remarkable, or part of a typical day. Either way, the key to practicing relational ethics is being able to see beyond your own taken-for-granted perspective and to consider the situation at hand from multiple vantage points.

Striving to understand other ethical worlds does not mean that you agree with them. You simply acknowledge that—as an adult, a youth worker, and a professional—you don't hold the one correct view of what is right and what it wrong. Furthermore, you embrace the complexity that exists within social interactions and recognize that there are often competing interests.

## The Real Dilemma: Youth Work in Unjust Spaces

> How we administer services forces youth to take on certain state-authored identities, submit to others' ideas about who they are and what they need. It's not ethical to participate in that without talking with them about it.
>
> *Angela, a youth worker*

Historically, youth work has been conceptualized as requiring the voluntary participation of young people. However, more and more in North America, youth work now occurs within the contexts of social services and the juvenile justice system. Often, youth are referred or mandated to a variety of services provided by youth workers.

Many of these youth workers are employed by the social service industry, and arguing about whether the work they do constitutes "real" youth work is not useful. The young people who receive these services may be vulnerable to exploitation and abuse. They may be homeless or at risk of becoming homeless. They may lack regular access to basic needs. They may have been targeted by law enforcement for petty crimes. They may live without the emotional and economic support of caring adults. While some young people may voluntarily seek social services, they must do so by entering agencies within the social service system. This typically means submitting to agency rules, procedures, and expectations in order to receive assistance. These expectations often require young people to meet standards of mainstream adult culture in order to fulfill their own basic needs for survival. Consequently, young people are often faced with compromising their dignity in order to get what they need.

## This Is Gonna Suck: Naming the Unjust Context

Being transparent about unjust circumstances by naming and acknowledging them is one important practice of relationally ethical youth work.

Mickella assists young people who are seeking housing. Before anyone starts to fill out what she believes is "an unreasonable amount of paperwork," she tells them, "This is gonna suck." Then she talks with them about the injustice and bureaucracy involved with addressing homelessness among young people. She often also talks with them about racism, adultism, and other injustices that impact their lives, and what the two of them are able to do together.

For example, young people who visit drop-in services typically have to conform to curfews and rules about drug or alcohol possession or use. While there may be some reasonable safety considerations behind rules such as these, from a housing-first perspective,[4] these rules would be an injustice, and thus would raise ethical concerns. Or consider a transgender or gender nonconforming youth who seeks shelter services. Shelter may require them to complete paperwork and use bathroom facilities that force them to choose "male" or "female" or use facilities according to the gender they were assigned at birth.

These issues raise important questions for youth workers, three of which are:

1. How do we practice relational responsibility, and ensure an ethic of care, with young people who may be either mandated to services, or who must submit to agency and institutional rules and procedures?
2. Is it ethical to help youth "get by" within an unjust system?
3. Is it ethical to refuse to help youth "get by" within an unjust system?

Answering these questions requires that we occupy a complex, both/and position. It's not possible to render absolute either/or answers about ethical practice. Rather, we need to acknowledge *both* the injustice of the broader systems serving youth *and* engage in practices of accountability and relational response-ability.

When we are working in contexts where young people are not participating voluntarily, or must compromise themselves in order to participate, it's crucial that we find ways to engage with them that center our ethics of care and response-ability. Examples of this include seeking young people's permission to ask questions or discuss certain topics; asking for their input and feedback on what we do and how we do it—and then integrating their ideas into our work; and finding ways for them to have some agency within confining circumstances.

Transparently acknowledging any unjust context is also important. For example, acknowledging the influence of white norms in a program's culture—rather than defending how things are done—can validate young people of color's experience of injustice and can remove some of the burden of the injustice from them. Once acknowledged, changing program practices and agency norms to reflect equity and accommodate cultural differences transforms ethical practice to a systemic level.

Many youth workers struggle with this question: *Is it ethical to provide services to young people within systems of injustice and institutional oppression?* Certainly, services provided by youth workers can keep young people alive and make their lives happier and more stable, even while they live in poverty, and (for example) while racism and misogyny swirl around them. On the one hand, when we take our ethics to a level of relational understanding, it may be difficult to consider that this is enough, that this is ethical. On the other, many people say, "That's just how things are. It's beyond me and youth work to fix the system and the world. I'm just here to help and support young people." But relational response-ability challenges us to see the interrelated effects of the prevailing discourses, the systems that maintain them, and the way that these impact the young people we work with—as well as the way we work with them. Indeed, centering ethics and the impact we have on others is challenging. Welcome to the complexity.

## Summary

A narrative approach to youth work involves relational ethics. This approach to ethics shifts from a focus on individual responsibility to relational response-ability—to how we respond within relationships and what the effects of these responses are. In addition, ethics moves to the center of our work and is reflected in all we do. This includes positioning, attending to and accounting for power, and addressing systemic issues of oppression.

Relational responsibility also reflects social construction's skepticism toward universality. This does not mean that we approach youth work with rampant relativism, in which anything goes. Rather, we evaluate any given situation based on how people are affected, not on whether we adhere to a particular rule. Rather than presume that dominant ethical standards are value neutral, we ask what values are inherent within our taken-for-granted ideas about right and wrong.

Modernist (i.e. traditional) ethical stances presume that we live in a world where uniformity, singularity, and consistency dominate. Until we acknowledge and embrace the multiplicity of worldviews and moral orders that are relationally constructed, we can harm the young people we work with by imposing what we claim are value-free ethical standards and practices upon them.

# Highlights

## The Shift: Individual to Relational Ethics

| *from* | *to* |
|---|---|
| Individual | Relational |
| Rules | Relationship |
| The universal (one size fits all) | Contextual, local, cultural understandings |
| The centering of professional knowledge and codes | The centering of young people's experience and cultural knowledge |
| The imposing of external ethics | Doing insider ethics relationally |
| Code of conduct | Relational stance |
| Certainty; agreement; correctness | Curiosity and understanding |
| Professional, dominant understandings at the moral center | Multiple perspectives valued |
| Value neutrality | Value-consciousness; an ethic of care |
| | *(Adapted from McNamee, 2009, 2015)* |

# Key Terms

1. **Relational responsibility:** Attentiveness to the very process of relating. Our dominant discourse of individual responsibility focuses on holding individuals responsible for their actions. In contrast, with relational responsibility, we shift our attention to what we construct in our relations with others, and how we construct particular moral orders.

2. **Ethic of care:** An ethic of care involves focusing our practice on the needs of people and relationships. Care is central to our work and not limited to responding to suffering.

3. **Centering ethics:** We make our ethics visible through the ways in which we do youth work. When we center our ethics, making them central to our practice, they permeate everything we do. They are not only for responding to dilemmas.

# Discussion Questions

1. "With great power comes great responsibility." (Although that quotation is often attributed to Spider-Man, it has a long history that predates the 1962 comic.) Think about the implications of this statement in the practice of youth work. As a youth worker, in what ways do you have power? What responsibilities come with that power? What have you observed about the relationship between the two? What thoughts do you have about that relationship?

2. If you were to write your own ethics mission statement, how would it read? In addition:

- What experiences, ideas, and/or people in your life influence or inform your ethics mission statement?
- What will young people notice about what you do that reflects your mission?
- What are two specific things you will do to bring your ethics mission into your work?
- What support do you need to do this? Whom do you need it from?
- What are some likely challenges or barriers to bringing your ethics mission into your work? How might you address these?

## Notes

1 This isn't just true of youth work; in all relationship-oriented professions, ethics have become largely a matter of rules and professional codes that serve primarily to avoid legal repercussions.
2 Consistency and fairness are of course aspects of many different discourses. The point here is that they are components of a behavioral framework—the particular framework that Jamal chose (without realizing that he chose it).
3 In fact, it is precisely because of concerns about power imbalances that most conventional ethical codes exist. These include rules about having relationships with youth outside of the youth work context, accepting gifts from youth, sharing personal information with youth, and so on.
4 A housing-first approach focuses on providing affordable, safe housing to people experiencing homelessness before they receive any or all other supportive services. This philosophy maintains that housing is a human right that all people deserve to have honored.

# PART II

# From Philosophical Groundwork to Praxis

Liberation is a praxis: the action and reflection of men and women upon their world in order to transform it.

*Paulo Freire*

I try to help black youth understand racial identity so they can navigate white supremacy and use their identities to transform society.

*Marjaan, a youth worker*

In the chapters that follow, we move into specific skills and practices for relationally engaged youth work. This does not mean that we leave the philosophical frameworks of Part I behind. On the contrary, it means that you will be introduced to practices that put into action the concepts introduced in the previous chapters. These are ways of working that reflect and are informed by constructionist philosophy and post-structural theory.

The practices in Chapters 4–9 will help you bring to life the ideas of social construction and post-structural theory through application and reflection. The integration of theory and practice through a process of reflection is known as *praxis*. Freire (1970) defines praxis as "reflection and action directed at the structures to be transformed" (p. 126). This common understanding of praxis belies the complexities and nuances embedded within the concept (see Carr, 1987; Schwandt, 2002; Stacey, 2001; and Tarlier, 2005), one which has its origins with Aristotle.

Jennifer White (2007) suggests an extension of praxis beyond this common understanding. She notes that praxis, as articulated by Freire (1970)—whose work in liberatory education is often central in the education of youth workers—embodies a relational/dialogical ethos and is intentionally political in its focus on transforming the world. Thus, she defines praxis as "ethical, self-aware, responsive, and accountable action" (p. 226).

White's extension offers an apt articulation of a constructionist take on praxis, one well-suited for the practices introduced in the following chapters. In particular, she encourages the "active integration of *knowing, doing, and being*" (p. 231, italics added), thus unhinging the problematic distinction between theory and practice. Furthermore, by "'verbing' the world of practice" (p. 231) (using *knowing* instead of knowledge, *doing* instead of skills, and *being* instead of self), White deliberately enters the constructionist action world of discursive production, fluidity, and nonessential identities. That is, rather than locating knowledge, skills, and the notion of "the self" inside youth workers, she places them in the social world as emergent social practices. This focus on knowing, doing, and being helps us answer the question: What do we do in practice?

The chapters in part two provide opportunities to cultivate a youth work praxis—the knowing, doing, and being—that is flexible and responsive to the relational contexts and cultural discourses that your work is situated in. These include the discourses that produce and sustain systems of white supremacy; patriarchy; capitalism; hetero-, homo-, and cis- normativity; classism; ableism; adultism; and nationalism. Accounting for context is central to this extended notion of praxis.

There's one more thing I need to mention about the ideas and practices in this part. It's important not to get caught up in the idea that these practices are in any way formulaic, or that I can or will provide an explicit "how-to" guide for approaching certain situations. That's the praxis part. The methods I offer and the examples I provide are not models to emulate or blueprints to follow. Rather, each is an example of how a constructionist stance and post-structural theory informed one relational engagement between a youth worker and a young person at one time. I invite you to reflect on these examples and generate ideas of your own about other possible paths of relational engagement.

# 4

# THAT'S A GOOD STORY

## Conversations that Do Things

Uttering a word is like striking a note on the keyboard of the imagination.
Ludwig Wittgenstein, *Philosophical Investigations*

There is not a script.

*Angela, a youth worker*

As discussed in Part I, social construction involves shifts from:

- the individual to the relational;
- an essentialist/internalized focus to an interest in the social world; and
- a descriptive view of language to an understanding of language as productive.

These shifts are known as the *narrative turn*. This orientation toward the relational and social means we concentrate our attention on *language practices*. This refers not only to words and speaking, but also to how we engage relationally with others and what comes from those engagements. Language practices are the relational stuff that contribute to making meaning and shaping lived experiences. The narrative turn serves as a guiding metaphor for the understanding that people organize and make sense of their lives through stories.

In youth work practice, the narrative turn invites a focus on conversation rather than on specific techniques. The focus on conversation affirms our understanding that we are actively participating in the making of stories, or *storying*. Our conversations with young people hold the discursive potential to construct and establish new stories, which they live as "realities." These conversations also can deconstruct and reconstruct stories that young people may be living, but that impose limitations or otherwise are problematic. In this chapter, we will consider ways to move from *stories to storying* through the conversations we have with young people.

## From Stories to Storying

> I want to have conversations that help them construct narratives and tell a story that lifts them up and recognizes their power as young black men.
>
> *Marjaan, a youth worker*

Every day, you probably engage in dozens, or even hundreds, of conversations—in person, over the phone, via text, on social media, or through web-based platforms. Then of course, there are the conversations in your head, with yourself and with others.

But what, exactly, is a conversation? What does it involve?

These may seem like weird questions, or at least ones that have obvious answers. Yet the actual answers are not that obvious or simple. How you answer these questions will likely depend on many things, including your social location, your lived experiences, a variety of cultural meanings about conversations, what you've learned and believe about communication, and your ideas about social interaction. Your answer might also include considerations of the context and intended purpose of the conversation.

While youth work occurs in many contexts and involves many kinds of activities and experiences, conversations are central to our work with young people. In a narrative approach, your job is that of a *conversationalist*: someone who partners in the cocreation of meaningful stories and experiences through collaborative conversations with young people.

In this era of curriculum-based approaches and an emphasis on one-size-fits-all models, it's tempting to look for a step-by-step manual that prescribes how to talk with young people—even if it involves repeating familiar, yet empty words that fail to be responsive to a young person's experience. These often end up being no size fitting anyone. The very fact that you are reading this book suggests that you place little faith in them.

When we instead focus on our relationship with young people and what emerges within the conversational moment, we don't have a script. Like jazz improvisation, however, it isn't that anything goes; rather, we engage responsively with others to create meaningful and preferred possibilities (Tilsen & Nylund, 2006). In jazz, the time signature, tempo, key, musical genre, and harmonic structure provide a framework for improvisation within which a new "song" (that is, the improvised melody) emerges. In narrative youth work, the social, cultural, and personal contexts that influence you and young people determine the landscape of your conversation, while the elements of story—*events, linked in sequence, across time, according to a plot* (Morgan, 2000)—come together to shape the emerging narratives of youths' lives.

Like jazz improvisation, social construction evokes novelty and possibility, and reflects what all participants come to the encounter with. We are not only concerned with what has been or what is; we are very interested in what could be. Good music is transcendent; good conversations make good stories.

---

**What is a Conversation?**

Have a conversation with some colleagues and discuss the following questions:

- What do people do in a conversation? What does their doing result in?
- What makes a conversation a conversation? Is there a kind of talk between or among people that is not a conversation?
- What's it like to be the person who is talking?
- What's it like to be the person who is listening?
- Would you answer the above two questions differently in different contexts?

---

How do we shape a conversation to one that embodies the generativity and creativity of relationally engaged youth work? What makes a conversation one that makes a good story, one that is *transformative*, one that gives "wing to the imaginative" (McNamee, 2000)? Here are some considerations to help you enter the realm of conversations that do things.

1. Situate individual story in cultural context

> Having a political grounding in my work is crucial—I have to pay attention to race, gender... all of it.
>
> *Eli, a youth worker*

As discussed in Chapter 1, our individual stories gain meaning and are legible through their relationship with the discourses that influence them. Situating young people's stories in context prevents the privatizing of social problems and burden of individualism (Tilsen, 2013). It also helps us bring forward richer, more complex stories, including stories of resistance and other counter-narratives to totalizing accounts. When we consider context and how discourses and power relations are shaping and influencing the youth we work with, we are better positioned to collaborate with them in telling stories that highlight their agency and acts of resistance.

2.  From monologue to dialogue

> Do it with me; I'm not telling you what to do.
>
> *Val, a youth worker*

Often, when we enter conversations with other people, we actually end up in a pattern of consecutive monologues: one person talks while the other waits for their turn to speak. How many of us remember being taught to "wait your turn to talk" when we were children? (What would it have been like if we were instead encouraged to "listen for points of connection and focus on understanding the other person?") If we're waiting our turn while someone else takes theirs, we're not really part of a shared project.

In monologue, the listener is positioned as the target of the speaker, both of whom operate as individuals. Dialogue, on the other hand, is a collaborative process that involves both a merging and an emergence of what happens. It requires an attuned responsiveness to the other person. This collaboration makes possible the emergence of new ideas—ideas that were unknown prior to the conversation.

3.  The listener as co-narrator

> I listen for those micro moments in conversations where it makes sense for me to fit in and help make something happen.
>
> *Jena B., a youth worker*

In dialogue, the listener shifts from being the target of the speaker to being a *co-narrator* (Bavelas, Coates, & Johnson, 2000) of the stories that are emerging. "Dialogue is a duet, not two solos" (Bavelas, Coates, & Johnsons, 2000, p. 942). Dialogue is a productive and creative enterprise of its own, a representation of the axiom, "the whole is greater than the sum of its parts." Co-narrators share the opportunity—*and responsibility*—to shape the dialogue.

What does it look like to be a co-narrator in practice? First, it requires that you *check yourself:* Remember that conversational partners are not waiting their turn to talk when listening. Chances are, if you are doing that, you are cueing up something to say that may not be in response to what is being said. Check yourself for an agenda—particularly one that reflects adultist or professionalized notions of what you should be saying or paying attention to. This will help you be engaged in what is actually happening in the conversation.

Secondly, as a co-narrator, you *check with the young person:* Ask them what *they* think about the conversation, what's being talked about, how it's going, etc. When you find yourself struck by something that's been said, check with the person to see if they share your interest in it, and if they'd like to hear your questions and thoughts about it.

Third, it's important to *reflect:* Tell the young person what the conversation evokes for you and what in it has captured your interest. Reflect out loud about the conversation—talk about the experience together.

Finally, as a co-narrator, *offer specific as well as generic responses:* We often help further conversations through *generic responses* (Bavelas, Coates, & Johnson, 2000), the things we do while listening that let people know we're tracking the conversation. We say "uh-huh" or "yeah," we nod, we tilt our head. These work with all kinds of conversations. But for many conversations they are not enough. Specific responses require that you understand the meaning of what's being said, that you demonstrate that understanding, and that you help further the conversation. This can involve completing a sentence or suggesting a word in a way that is meaningful to the speaker, or asking a question that opens up the discussion, or causes the other person to say, "That's a great question; I hadn't thought of that!"

4.  Understanding and curiosity vs. resolution and certainty

He didn't expect me to be interested in his street life.

*Mikella, a youth worker*

Our conventional ideas and practices of communication promote a focus on "getting somewhere"—that is, coming to an agreement, a resolution, or an answer. We can easily find ourselves focusing narrowly on problem solving, or trying to convince others of what they should think or do. We want to push toward answers, fixes, and resolutions. Yet this often communicates the opposite of understanding.

In genuine dialogue, however, our commitment is to seek to *understand the other.* This means that we cultivate appreciation and empathy for young people's experiences and attend to the meanings that they make of their experiences. This understanding fosters engagement and connection, both of which are requisite for conversations that do things.

These conversations rarely include certainty or declarative statements that function as truth claims. These stifle conversation and connection. Conversely, generative curiosity unfolds a multiplicity of possibilities and helps keep the conversation—and the relationship—going. We can show up with curiosity, engage the imaginative, and ask (and encourage) interesting questions rather than proceed with certainty and seek (and settle for) answers. When we do, we enter the world of storying and re-storying (also known as re-authoring), where transformative narratives unfold into lived realities. *We become interested in what might be possible.*

Consider the examples that follow of transformative conversations. What became possible? How would you describe where the conversation started and where it moved to? What was the process of storying, and what stories emerged? What did these conversations *do?*

1.  Val described meeting Anthony, a 20-year-old cisgender gay black man who has many service providers involved in his life. In her first meeting with him, Anthony told her about his relationships with these professionals, including: case managers, mental health and medical professionals,

outreach workers, and housing advocates. Through his lengthy engagement with these professionals, Anthony had come to refer to himself as "crazy" because of the concerns they have about his unconventional interests, his "unstable lifestyle," and his eccentric social ways. Val was struck by how Anthony had assumed the totalizing identity of mental illness as his primary defining characteristic. After listening to Anthony's account and asking some questions about his interests and hopes for the future, she asked if she could see some of his artwork, which he had briefly mentioned. Val was blown away with Anthony's unique creativity and vision. "Anthony," Val said. "You're not crazy. You're a genius." Anthony straightened up in his chair and continued an enthusiastic conversation with Val about his art, what it meant to him, and how it helped him go through a world that didn't see him as he'd like to be seen. "I'm convinced," Val said, "that I was meeting someone that none of the other professionals in his life had met, simply because we had this conversation. I've never had a conversation like that in 20 years—it felt spiritual, like the conversation was doing something as we talked. And I think Anthony felt like he was re-meeting a part of himself that he had assumed had to be dismissed. He finally felt validated."

2. Marjaan talks about how he, as a black man, will invite black youth into conversations that call out the whiteness of the social service systems they are involved in (including the agency where Marjaan worked). Together, he and the young people identify ways in which they see whiteness operating. They share their strategies of resistance—small but significant ways in which they stand against whiteness, assert their identities, exercise agency, and maintain their dignity within a broader culture and system of "services" that routinely impose norms of whiteness. Some of the young people rap or create visual art projects that tell their stories of resistance, thus reclaiming their storytelling rights. These new narratives cast the youth as courageous, creative, and capable, a powerful counter-narrative to the one often upheld by white supremacy.

3. A large youth-serving agency asked me to do a training on working with queer and transgender youth. The workshop would be part of a conference the agency was hosting. I agreed to do the training on three conditions: (1) that I would take an intersectional approach and emphasize the experiences of queer and trans youth of color, (2) that queer and trans youth of color could be my co-presenters, and (3) that my co-presenters would be compensated at the same rate that I was. After discussion about the assumptions embedded within "professionalism," the agency agreed. In the workshop, we situated ourselves so that my co-presenters were positioned as the experts on queer and trans youth, while I was positioned as an interviewer. I asked questions that brought out their recommendations for youth workers, including their concerns about (and their critiques of) how queer and trans youth are treated by service providers. One of their recommendations was that more queer and trans youth need to be hired as youth workers serving queer and trans youth.

In each of these examples, a youth worker situated the conversation within a discursive context that directly influenced young people. Val, in nuanced fashion, acknowledged and resisted the discourse of psychological normativity. Marjaan directly named white supremacy and contextualized young black men's experience within it. I exposed normative and adultist assumptions about professionalism and the problematic limitations of a non-intersectional approach to youth work. Thus, we each acknowledged the contextual and political influences operating in the lives of youth. Furthermore, each of us focused on the transformative: things that could be possible rather than probable; that were generative and expansive rather than finite and limiting; and that centered the skills, abilities, hopes, and preferences of the young people, some of which had previously been hidden in the margins.

These examples also highlight the importance of *resistance* in transformative dialogue and re-authoring identity narratives. This is especially critical with marginalized youth. Remember from Chapter 2: *where there is power there is resistance*. Giving voice to and witnessing youth resistance to normative and pathologizing discourses that specify and restrict available identity conclusions is imperative. Through conversations that honor and bring forward youth resistance to anything that limits what could be possible, youth can begin to imagine new alternatives and experience unrealized potential.

---

## Re-Storying Practice

In Chapter 2, I asked you to identify a totalizing description about yourself. *In the center of a piece of paper, write down your answers to these questions:*

- What story does that description circulate about you?
- Who does it require you to be?
- What events does it feature, what is the timeline of this story, and what plot unfolds?
- How is it circulated and in what ways do you live this story?

*In the margins of the paper, write your answers to these questions:*

- What are some contextual factors that the story of the totalizing description fails to consider?
- What assumptions does this story rely on?
- What events does it select out in order to maintain its veracity? When have there been exceptions to this story?
- What story might these exceptions have to tell about you?

---

### #FergusonSyllabus Question

How are oppressive stories about marginalized youth circulated, and how are youth's stories of resistance erased? In what ways do youth end up "living" these stories?

When you engage in transformative conversations, youth are not the only people impacted by them. How are you impacted when you participate in the re-storying of a transformative conversation that honors young people's resistance?

---

## Storying Life After a Death: Making a Conversation Matter When All Seems Lost

> Sometimes we have to sit there and figure it out with the youth.
>
> *Jena B., a youth worker*

In October 2002, I was facilitating a youth leadership retreat with two other youth workers, my friends Val[1] and Aundaray. A group of about 30 juniors and seniors from the Minneapolis Public Schools, along with a handful of their teachers, had gathered at a beautiful nature center for a day of activities and conversations about power and privilege. These young people were the social justice super heroes of their respective schools.

Nearing the conclusion of an intense, fun, intimate, and hopeful day, one of the teachers told me that she needed to talk with me for a moment. After letting the group know I'd be right back, I followed her into the hallway. The teacher told me that she had just received a call from a school administrator. A public figure and champion of social justice had died in a plane crash. Senator Paul Wellstone[2] was an important role model and inspiration for many of the students. His death would be all over the news and the school was hoping that we would make space to address it with the students while they were in a structured environment.

Quickly, Val, Aundaray, and I had to sort through how we might approach this situation. We knew that most of the students at the retreat would be devastated, and the three of us were struggling to keep ourselves from going under in a tidal wave of feelings. After consulting together, we gathered the young people in a circle. I shared the crushing news with the group.

The grief was palpable, the tears unrestrained, and the disbelief burdensome. Students and adults leaned into each other—literally and figuratively—for comfort and support.

Several minutes went by while we held space for the river of feelings that rushed through the group. Finally, I decided to speak: "You know, you guys are doing the work that Senator Wellstone inspired you to do. That's why you came today. All day today, you've been doing that work. And you'll be doing it tomorrow, and the next day, and the next." I said most of this through my own tears—it was breaking my heart how much their hearts were breaking.

I wasn't sure where this would go, or if it was the right thing to say or the right time to say it. There were a few looks of mild confusion on young people's faces. In addition, a few faces brightened—just a little bit—with the light of purpose and hope.

Slowly, as if the group was collectively navigating the ruins of their collapsed assumptions about the constancy and continuity of their world, we weaved together a conversation. As we talked, I asked some of the following questions in response to what was emerging from the group:[3]

- What do you think the grief you're feeling says about your relationship with Senator Wellstone and what he stood for?
- What connection do you make between the passion that brought you here today and the depth of the sadness you're feeling right now?
- What do you need others to know about what Senator Wellstone means to you as young people and in your roles as social justice leaders in your schools?
- What are some of your favori̇        ̇ies about Senator Wellstone?
- If he could tell a story abȯ          ̇ would you like it to be?
- What role did he play in yȯ            today?
- If we had asked you earlier ̇            ̇ve knew that we would lose him today, "What would Senatȯ           ̇ant you to take away from today?" what would you have said?
- How is that the same as, or different fṙ           would say now, after learning that he's gone?
- We've talked today about being sustained ̇          ̇rted in your social justice work. How are your ideas about what ẏ   ̇need to do to continue this work affected by Senator Wellstone's death? What do you need from each other to do this?
- Some of you have mentioned wanting to do something to honor him. What ideas do you have for this? What have you worked on today that might inspire you in turning those ideas into realities and/or in coming up with other ideas? How can you be resources for each other in this?
- How might the relationships you've made today be something that you turn to when you are remembering him or want to continue this work?

These questions[4] were part of a purposeful effort to re-story their experience. The intentions behind these questions, and the conversation they made possible, included:

- Validate and honor youth's complex feelings of grief, fear, and confusion.
- Invite multiple meanings to be made of the expressions of those emotions.

- Nurture youth's capacity for standing in the dark chasm of despair, while also calling up the possibility of making something of the despair.
- Acknowledge their fear of uncertainty, as well as their own histories—and potential futures—of courage.
- Validate their personal and collective sense of defeat—without succumbing to defeatism.
- Highlight and support the connections that were cultivated within the group, and invite them to consider ways to maintain them.

The conversation also provided a gentle invitation for these young people to imagine a time to come when they would carry this painful moment forward with intention and purpose, and create something hopeful from it. This invitation was not one to "move on" or "get over" their grief. Rather, it was an invitation to consider what their feelings suggested might be important and meaningful for them to do. It was also an invitation to story their experience into the future where possibilities existed for them to live into their values, intentions, and aspirations.

This transformative process of storying is an example of *social poetics*.[5] Social poetics refers to a dialogue of transformation, emergent meanings, new possibilities, and resistance to the all too common silencing of young people. When we take a narrative approach to youth work that is firmly grounded in relational ethics, attuned to power operations, and open to a multiplicity of meanings, we open up many conversational paths. This reflects Deleuze and Guattari's (1987) idea of "lines of flight," which spotlight the evocative and transformative rather than the definitive and static.

In practice, this means that we replace what are often the predictable, prescribed techniques of the professional—what McNamee (2000) calls "the constraints of traditional forms of practice" (p. 146)—with an evocative sense of enchantment or wonder (Sanders, 2007) that unfolds through relational connection. In the previous example, a predictable (modernist) practice would have been to facilitate an experience that privileged individual expression of feelings. We would assume a universalized understanding of these feelings. Part of this assumption would be situating those feelings internally in each young person, rather than socially within the relational realm. It is within the relational space that the transformative becomes available.

Transformative conversations are not reserved for an amazing, indescribable moment. Your encounter with young people needn't be fraught with grief like it was in my story. And transformation isn't available only to youth—youth workers are touched as well. Transformative conversations impact everyone engaged in this kind of creative relational encounter. At the center of these conversations is the crucible of people coming together to create something new and hopeful. These are profound relational opportunities. These are the makings of good stories.

## Summary

When we focus on language practices we enter the relational world of conversation and storying. In collaboration with youth, we are improvising our way to a good story—one which allows young people to occupy their rightful place as author in their own life and which affords them the most meaningful ways of being in the world. We abandon the cultural penchant for certainty, agreement, and resolution, and instead enthusiastically show up with curiosity, strive to understand, and value generative possibilities.

Transformative conversations are evocative and inspired by the wonder of possibility. We orient our conversational compasses so that we travel relationally and dialogically—often we travel off road, taking unexpected paths, some of which may not be authorized by conventional practice. This willingness to explore conversationally allows meaning and purpose to emerge and re-authoring of new narratives to ensue. Our willingness to engage in the unexpected and honor resistance to oppressive norms helps young people stretch the bounds of their imaginations and abilities.

## Highlights

### From Monologue to Dialogue

| Monologue | Dialogue |
|---|---|
| Story | Storying |
| Take turns | Listener as co-narrator |
| Resolution/agreement/answers | Understanding/meaning/questions |
| Certainty | Curiosity |
| Mechanics/Script | Poetics/Improvisation |

## Key Terms

1. **Dialogue:** From a constructionist perspective, dialogue is a conversation characterized by a collaborative relational process in which all participants contribute to an emergent conversation by responding to each other. As such, dialogue is a type of conversation that stands in contrast to *monologue*.

2. **Social Poetics:** Narrative practitioners use social poetics to describe relationally engaged conversations that make the transformative possible. *Social* refers to relational (as opposed to individual) and *poetics* is contrasted to mechanics/techniques and speaks to the improvisatory and imaginative quality of the conversations.

3. **Transformative:** For our purposes, transformative refers to relationally engaged youth work that (1) fosters the possibility of moving beyond current understandings, (2) leverages the imaginations of youth and youth workers, and (3) ushers in new and meaningful ways of being that stand in resistance to the constraints of normativity.

## Discussion Questions

1. How do you think about your role in conversations that do things? What comes to mind when you think about improvising?
2. In what ways does thinking about *listener as co-narrator* change how you approach conversations? What is challenging about this? What does it make possible?
3. Think about a recent conversation you've had that was a monologue—each person "waiting their turn" to speak and not really responding to each other in a way that generated something new between/among them. What are some things you could have said or done differently that may have changed this experience to a transformative dialogue?
4. If you were to re-author a story about yourself, what would it be? What about re-storying this part of your life appeals to you? Where would you start? Who in your life knows about you in the alternative story you seek to pull from the margins?

## Notes

1 This is the same Val as the person whose comments appear throughout the book.
2 It isn't important if Senator Wellstone (and his untimely death) is significant to you; understanding that he was significant to these youth is important. I am not asking you to connect with the story of Senator Wellstone and his death; I am asking you to connect with the process through which we engaged the youth in this difficult moment.
3 I am writing about an experience that I had many years ago. I cannot provide a precise word-for-word account of the entire group conversation. I can, however, offer an account in the spirit of what happened, an elaboration of the story of the experience shaped by the pieces I've remembered and retold.
4 Chapter 7 will focus on the art and craft of asking questions and will provide greater grounding in understanding the questions presented in this chapter.
5 *Social* refers to the relational and *poetics* stands in contrast to mechanics, or technical. For more on social poetics, the reader is referred to McNamee (2000) and Sanders (1999, 2007, 2014).

# 5

# CAN YOU HEAR ME NOW?
# LISTENING, REALLY LISTENING

An appreciative listener is always stimulating.

*Agatha Christie*

Listening is a whole-body experience.

*Emily, a youth worker*

Chapter 4 began by asking the question, *what is a conversation?* In this chapter, we will take up a fundamental aspect of conversations: listening.

By focusing on listening as an isolated skill, I do not intend to promote listening as a discrete and technical application, disembodied from relational engagement. Parsing out different facets of dialogue facilitates taking a close-up look at the parts of the whole, while still holding firmly to the notion that *the whole is greater than the sum of its parts*. Indeed, the concepts and approaches that follow invite you to regard listening as one part that works in relationship with other parts to come together to make the "whole" that is a relationally engaged conversation.

In jazz improvisation, performers listen and respond in the moment, highlighting and developing certain rhythmic, harmonic, and melodic themes. That's what happens in good storying, too: listeners bring out and make room for certain ideas to gain narrative traction through their responses.

One would be hard-pressed to find a youth worker who would disagree with the contention that being good at listening is a prerequisite for the work. The centrality of listening in the practice of youth work makes answering questions such as the following even more important: *What does listening do? What is its purpose and what does it make possible? How is listening understood and practiced from a narrative approach?*

Before we consider these questions, take a moment to think about a time when you felt listened to. What is it that the person listening did or did not do that left you with the experience of feeling listened to?

When I ask this question to youth about their experiences with youth workers, they often say, *"they got me, they understood."* When I ask them how they know that the youth worker got them, young people say, *"because they said things or asked questions that fit how I want to be understood."* Indeed, although we often point to what we do while *not* talking, it is what we say *while speaking* that demonstrates the quality of our listening. The two go hand in hand.

Now, think about a time when you felt *not* listened to. Often, we characterize these experiences by things that demonstrate inattentiveness or disinterest on the part of the person who is supposed to be listening: being distracted, interrupting, doing other things, etc. When we feel we've not been listened to, we also experience not being understood. We all have had experiences when we just didn't feel the other person got us and *what matters* to us. Their lack of understanding and dismissiveness are reflected in what they said or did not say in response. In this chapter, we will focus on cultivating abilities of listening, or *listen-ability*, that emphasize understanding and responding in ways that center what matters to youth.

## Moving Beyond "Active Listening"

> I'm not just listening to the words coming out of their mouths. I'm listening to systems and discourses.
>
> *Quinn, a youth worker*

In youth work, we often talk about "active listening." This idea reflects certain assumptions about the practice of listening. However, it doesn't tell us much about what to *do* when listening.

Let's look at some of the assumptions and limitations of the idea of "active listening." Active listening implies that there is such a thing as "passive listening." Building on the idea of listener as co-narrator introduced in Chapter 4, the shift to dialogue unhinges the rigid parameters around speaker and listener. In this sense, the listener is always an active contributor—even when sitting quietly—to the conversation that unfolds between participants. When we consider concepts such as discursive production, dialogue, and listener as co-narrator, the either/or of active/passive gives way to a more nuanced, contextual, and relationally situated understanding of listening.

Another limitation of the "active listening" notion is that value is placed on whatever is constituted as "active" (a purely subjective and contingent evaluation), while "passive" (an equally subjective and contingent description) is viewed as less valuable. Paré (2013) notes that "listening...is never a passive task, and even in silence, there's a lot going on" (p. 87). What "goes on" while we're listening reflects our philosophical stance and relational positioning. It also informs *what* we respond to and *how* we respond. This includes what we do and don't listen for, our thoughts and reactions to those things, the discourses we notice and privilege, and how our identities (that is, the social locations we occupy) influence the "lenses" that we listen through.

---

## Describing Listening

Here is a variety of possible ways to describe *listening*. What do each of these descriptions evoke for you?

1. Engaged listening
2. Curious listening
3. Attuned listening
4. Attentive listening
5. Generous listening
6. Thoughtful listening
7. Deep listening
8. Reflective listening
9. Mindful listening
10. Affirmative listening
11. What other kinds of listening or ways to describe listening resonate with you?

How do you describe the kind of listening you aspire to do as a youth worker? What are some considerations you take into account when you think about the practice of listening?

---

How can we be attuned to all that's going on while listening? Jennifer White's (2007) reflexive praxis work presented in the introduction of Part II helps us cultivate an intentional awareness of discourses and power relations. Accounting for these in "real time" while we're in conversation allows us to navigate our listening toward possibilities and away from limitations. Some questions we can ask ourselves are listed as follows. As you read them, consider how they reflect and support the premise (discussed in Chapter 4) that people organize their lives and make meaning of their world through stories.

- How do my identities/social locations influence what I'm attending to and how I'm reacting? What are the impacts of this? (power relations)
- Who do I need to be for this young person (these young people)? How do they want me to show up? (relational responsiveness)

- Who does the dominant story require them to be? ' ... >es it require me to be? (story development and influence of dis'
- What limitations does the current stor ... .mpose? (story development and influence of discour'
- What are the cultural norms that ... .rsion? (power relations and influence of discourse)
- When could things develop ... .other? (story development)
- When could I be inquiring abc ... present/future? (story development)
- Where might different underst. .dings be located? (story development, alternative discourses)
- How is what they're describing important, meaningful, or significant to them? (relational responsiveness)
- How can we keep the conversation going and generating new and meaningful stories? (story development, relational responsiveness)

What did you notice about these questions? How would you describe them and what they do? Which of these are most like the questions that you already ask yourself or that you would like to reflect on?

I also draw on queer theory[1] (Butler, 1990, 2004; Foucault, 1978; Halberstam, 2005; Sedgewick, 1990; Warner, 1999) to help me reflect on discourses that are influencing me, the youth, and our conversation. Queer theory is especially helpful when talking about power relations and identity. Here are some of the critical queer theory-informed questions that address power relations and the influence of cultural discourses that impact identity:

- What are the cultural rules (gender and sexuality specifications, Eurocentric assumptions, notions of normal, middle-class values, etc.) that are requiring certain ways of being and prohibiting others?
- Whom do these rules serve?
- Who is included and who is excluded when these rules are enforced?
- Who has the power to define the rules?
- How are the rules policed?
- How do these rules change over time and across cultures?

*(Adapted from Doty, 1993)*

These are questions to consider both during your conversation and outside of times of engagement with youth. They are intended to help you continually consider what influences you and what you are positioned to hear.

In addition to these lens-adjusting questions, constructionists also draw on the idea of the *inner dialogue,*[2] which is derived from the work of Bakhtin (1981, 1984). From a constructionist stance that emphasizes story development, collaboration, nonessentialist identity, honoring of local knowledges, and generating multiple possibilities, we cultivate an inner dialogue that is flexible, fluid, and responsive. That ways to show up and many "voices" we can use. When we have a variety ways to be with youth, we are better positioned to listen from a variety of perspectives.

Thus, our inner dialogue requires that we continuously ask ourselves, *how can I show up in ways that invite youth to participate in a conversation that would be most meaningful for them? What voice do I use?* For example, we may consider the voice of possibility rather than certainty, the voice of curiosity rather than finality, the voice of a trusted friend rather than of a distant authority. We seek and try on different voices in response to what we hear; we take on a particular voice to invite youth to say more, so that we may listen more. This is a constant and recursive negotiation of relational engagement and understanding.

## Do You Hear What I Hear? Adjusting Our Listening Frequency

> I try not to listen to what other adults think about a youth before I can listen to them on their own terms.
>
> *Jenna D., a youth worker*

Why do we listen? What is its purpose and what do we hope will come from it?

It's not a stretch to say that listening is vital to relationship-building and that relationships thrive (in part) on understanding. In fact, I often say that the first imperative of listening is to understand. Making understanding rather than agreement your priority in conversations is an ethical stance that reflects an important shift in dialogical approaches to youth work. Pro tip: *understanding does not mean endorsement.* It does mean that you are willing to suspend what you think or believe in order to further your relationship with young people.

As youth workers, we want to understand the youth we work with and we want them to feel understood by us. But understanding *what* and according *to whom?* Michael White (2007) suggests that asking questions to expose power relations serves to "locate knowledge in social, cultural, political, and historical contexts" (p. 234) and questions taken-for-granted assumptions embedded within prevailing discourses. Unpacking these assumptions cultivates our capacity for listen-ability by positioning us to understand outside of the limitations of normative discourses such as white supremacy, patriarchy, hetero- and homonormativity, ableism, and cissexism.

Walter and Peller (2000) point out that within the modernist tradition that privileges professional expertise over local knowledge, professionals tend to listen in terms of the constructs that inform their professional perspectives. Historically, youth work has sought to challenge the imposition of professionalized and institutionalized knowledges. This has become more challenging as youth work is being done more and more within the social service industry where professional expertise is privileged. Thus, youth workers—and their inner dialogues—reflect the influences of professional ideas about young people.

For example, youth work often uses a developmental lens to understand a young person's refusal to accept our assistance managing a challenging situation. The professional understanding reached through a developmental lens interprets this refusal as a universal condition that assumes all teenagers are destined to "power struggle" with authorities. We may understand this developmental stage in a way that is dismissive of the meaning that young person assigns to their rejection of our help. Yet, our understanding—what we take from our listening—"does not necessarily equate with the client's[3] feeling understood" (Walter & Peller, 2000, p. 54). Consequently, this listening may not lead to the understanding of what matters to those who we are supposed to be listening to.

What does listening look like from a constructionist stance? What practices of listening do we engage in within a narrative approach?

While individualism and modernist discourses of professionalism emphasize listening for "The Truth," social construction and post-structural theories orient us toward a multiplicity of truths. This shift situates individuals in context, taking into consideration the multiple factors that shape and influence who they are and how they experience the world. We shift from listening to "figure out" to listening to understand in young people's terms. We check our responses if they smack at all of "adult knows best."

Recall from Chapter 2 the discussion about positioning ourselves as decentered and influential. When we take this position, we listen in ways that allow us to understand what matters to young people. In the example of the young

---

### #FergusonSyllabus Question

How do you cultivate listen-ability that communicates compassion for, understanding of, and interest in youths' worlds, especially when those worlds differ from yours? What are some issues related to how power is operating when listening across differences that you want to consider?

Sometimes, we may share common identities or social locations with some of the youth we engage with. At times, we may also have some of the same life experiences or interests as they do. Often, we will be engaging across differences, be they around race, gender, sexuality, class, culture, ability, religion, life experiences, etc. This is the challenging beauty and beautiful challenge of relational engagement: cultivating understanding of and appreciation for youth despite dissimilarities, and perhaps even disagreements. This requires us to engage critically with discourses that shape our view of the world. It also calls on us to suspend our assumptions and beliefs to honor youth whose ways of being differ from ours.

person who rejects our assistance, we would adjust our listening lens to be attuned to what's important to them about refusal of assistance rather than imposing a universalized interpretation (in this example, age-appropriate power struggle) rendered from a professionalized discourse.

Thus, we listen for ways to connect to what matters to young people by cultivating understanding and appreciation of what has meaning for them in context. This is the first imperative of listening: To understand The Other as other (Sampson, 2008).

## Absent but Implicit: Listening for the Unspoken Story

> I listen for the things she hopes and the things she wants to try.
>
> *Emily, a youth worker*

How do we listen in ways that help us understand what matters to youth? Michael White's (2000) concept of *absent but implicit* offers us hopeful ways of responding to this central question.

Drawing on the work of Bateson (1980) and Derrida (1978), White points out that we can't talk about *what is* without understanding *what is not* (Cary, Walther, & Russell, 2009). For example, if I say, "the mattress in the cabin is too hard" I need to have some experience of "soft" to make sense of hard. The story of the hard mattress gets privileged while my experiences with softness get relegated to the margins in this tale of pained sleep. Put another way, making sense of experiences requires that we make distinctions between what is present and what is not (Derrida, 1978). My experiences with "soft" are *absent but implicit*—they are not present in this conversation, but they are implied because they are necessary to make sense of "hard."

Thus, for experiences to be legible to us, we set them apart from other experiences that we've already made meaning of. It is through this contrast to experiences that "already have meaning to us and which have already been described or categorized in some way" (Carey, Walther, & Russell, 2009, p. 321) that I can declare the cabin mattress as hard: I have had experience with soft sleeping surfaces. (And these soft mattresses may feel hard compared to other mattresses, or, in another person's experience!)

What does this have to do with youth work practice? How is this connected to the practice of listening? To answer these questions, let's move from mattresses to expressions and experiences that may show up in conversations with young people. Consider the expressions in the list that follows and identify the absent but implicit expression:

- Hopelessness
- Sadness

- Mistrust
- Embarrassment

Noticing the absent but implicit requires that we ask ourselves "what is *not present* in each experience? What is this expression distinct from?" Using

---

### Absent but Implicit/Double Listening Practice

Listening for the absent but implicit requires us to listen on the "other side" of what is expressed. Asking yourself, *"what does it sound like is desired or preferred?"* is a good first step toward hearing what's on the other side of an expression. Here are some possible ways to understand the absent but implicit for each expression. Can you think of others?

| Present and Explicit | Absent but Implicit |
| --- | --- |
| Hopelessness | Hope |
| Loneliness | Connection |
| Worries | Assurance |
| Sadness | Joy |
| Anger | Justice |
| Guilt | Accountability |
| Fear | Safety |

Once you're able to use double listening, the next st[...] g a question that invites youth to speak to the absent but implic[...] some example questions to ask in response to the statement. V[...] her questions you can think of that invite a conversation about w[...] to the young person speaking?

| Statement | Double Listening Response |
| --- | --- |
| I'm so frustrated. | What expectations aren't being met? |
| I'm super angry. | What unfairness is anger protesting? |
| You don't understand. | When have you felt understood and what did that make possible? |
| I don't trust my team. | What's important about trust that matters to you? |
| This activity is too scary. | What do you want to keep safe? |
| That class is stupid. | What did you hope for or expect from the class? |
| I quit. It's not worth trying anymore. | Before now, what made your efforts worth it? |

the first step of deconstruction (Derrida, 1978), we turn to the *binary opposite*—the term or expression that is opposed to the central expression. In the previous list, these opposites might be expressed as: hope, happiness, trust, and pride. These are the absent but implicit meanings embedded within the present and explicit. By tuning our listening in to these absent but implicit expressions, we can shift the conversational focus to what matters to the young person speaking.

Michael White (2000) calls the practice of tuning into the absent but implicit *double listening*. When we "doubly listen," we attend not only to the dominant story presented to us, but also to the expression on the other side of that story. Double listening opens the door for alternative stories by zeroing in on what matters to young people and providing pathways for generative narratives. When we listen for what's on the other side of the experience that's been described, we can inquire about the significance and meaning of the absent but implicit. Here, in what has yet to be spoken, lies a wealth of stories well worthy of a good listen.

## Listening to Things Besides Words

Listening goes beyond hearing information.

*Emily, a youth worker*

When we're organized around stories and listening for what matters, we attend to more than the words that come out of young people's mouths. What young people *do* is also a site of meaning to be made. We seek to understand and contextualize youths' actions in ways that honor their intentions and agency. Attending in this way means we "listen" to the actions and practices that young people take up in ways that situate them in space and time, bearing in mind influential discourses and lived experiences. Listening to actions may require that we suspend assumptions based on prevailing discourses and actively seek to understand what the act means to the youth.

For example, when a black transgender girl dresses in fancy high-femme clothes while participating in an urban gardening program, we can "listen" for the significance of her expression of gender within a transmisogynist and racist culture by asking ourselves, *what is important to her about dressing up while getting dirty?* Or, when a young person from a single-parent family frequently skips school to stay home with an ailing grandparent, we can "listen" to their act of staying home within the discourse of behavioral choice and normative ideas about family structure and roles, or we can hear it as an embodiment of what matters to them: their relationship with an important elder. These are just two examples of "listening" to actions in ways that allow young people ownership of their storytelling rights.

## Listening Beyond Words: From Models to Meaning

Jena B. tells the following story of "listening" to the actions of two young people in ways that decenter professional understandings and discourses to make room to listen to what mattered to Addie and Max.

"Addie and Max, both 19, shared an apartment in subsidized housing. They had a lot of unstructured time while they were both looking for work. During this time, they started building a model city out of pipe cleaners, popsicle sticks, and other stuff they scavenged from the garbage or received from drop-in centers. Before I met with them, their housing case manager said, 'whatever you do, don't let them suck you into a conversation about the model houses they're building and pipe dreams about being architects. They need to focus on getting jobs.'

When I met with them, I showed interest in their model and asked about it. What I heard is how doing this helped them feel like they were doing something while they looked for jobs. Making the model was a creative and intellectual activity, it kept them from fussing at each other because they worked together on it, it got them out of bed, and it got them to places where were job search resources and supplies for the model. It also had to do with Addie's childhood dream of being an architect. I wouldn't have understood that if I'd just shown up like, 'dudes, we gotta talk about upping your job search game.' That's what their case manager would do, and they totally shut her out. So, we talked about the model and what it meant for them to spend time on it—and I mean they would spend several hours a day on it, and they were very detailed about it. That model called into question everything adults typically thought about them because it showed that they weren't lazy, that they had skills and a desire to work, and that it was important to them to make something that they could take pride in."

## Listening is Dialogical: Speaking to Listen

> I have to say something, ask some questions, that help me listen.
>
> *Jena B., a youth worker*

By now it's probably quite clear that listening is not only about sitting quietly while young people talk. A narrative approach to youth work involves a more complex understanding of the co-influential relationship between speaker and listener in addition to an emphasis on understanding. A major implication of adjusting our listening lens to amplify what matters to young people is that our responses shift as well. In fact, the *purpose* of speaking changes. Hoffman (2002) introduces the notion of *speaking to listen*. Speaking to listen means that, when we're engaged in dialogue in which we take a decentered but influential position, much of what we say serves the purpose of making room for youth to say more. The examples below are conversational practices that you undoubtedly use. What may be new is thinking about them as part of a practice of *speaking to listen*:

- Asking for clarification:
  ○ When you say, "it was the best day ever," do you mean here at camp or in your whole life?
- Asking for more details:
  ○ Can you say more?
- Seeking confirmation of meaning:
  ○ Am I getting you right that you're feeling really proud about it, or are you saying something else?
- Repeating back to allow reflection:
  ○ Okay, you said, "I had the best day ever after we played dodgeball and then just chilled in the dining hall."
- Asking questions that help develop a preferred story[4]
  ○ What could this kind of day of playing games and chillin' lead to in the future for you?

I offer these as brief examples of skills you've likely used before. As you move forward with them, try to notice what your inner dialogue is and how you may be employing these skills differently as you focus on your positioning. The idea of speaking to listen not only invites us to reimagine the acts of speaking and listening, but it also furthers the notion of dialogue and the generativity of co-construction. Youth and youth workers listening and speaking together hold the possibility of constructing good stories worthy of a good listen.

## Note-Taking as a Listening Practice

In many youth work contexts, documentation is often a required and rarely enjoyable part of the job. This is especially true as youth work becomes more and more institutionalized as a part of the social service industry. Yet, it is possible to approach note-taking as a listening practice, one that facilitates conversation while also working to deinstitutionalize the task of documentation itself.

*(Continued)*

As a listening practice, taking notes is a helpful way to keep track of important things that are said. You may want to revisit something or ask for clarification about it later. Having a few notes jotted down helps you continue listening while keeping track of things that catch your attention in a way that doesn't require interrupting.

How you do this—and why you do it—makes all the difference as to whether note-taking comes off as something that creates distance or supports collaboration. This is about positioning and transparency. It is also about honoring young people's author-ity rather than perpetuating the privileging of adult/professional knowledges and expertise.

For example, you can let young people know that it's important to you to understand what matters to them, and you'd like to take some notes so you can keep track of that. Ask them if that's okay, answer any questions they may have, and—this is a deinstitutionalizing part—tell them you want their help in knowing what to write down.

Take notes together. Offer choices of pen colors. You can write on a white board and take a picture of it with their phone if they have one (I call these "out loud notes"). Make lists, draw pictures, compose cheers, jingles, mottos, or bumper stickers. If you've had a chat while shooting hoops or walking in the woods, when you get back from the activity, sit down together and make a list of the things you both think worthy of remembering. When you do that, youth get to tell their stories again, and you get to listen. And you may end up with a poem, piece of art, or slogan to live by.

## Summary

Youth work often happens on the go: in the streets, in a noisy school hallway, around a quiet campfire at night, or on the basketball court. Cultivating listenability means we make a relational space that allows us to partner with youth in the cocreation of dialogue. This nurtures a connection and deepens relationships. We are always active when we listen—even when we silently bear witness to youths' stories. We are accounting for power relations and positioning, attending to discourses, and minding our inner dialogue as a conversational compass.

Speaking is necessary for listening—it is in our responses that we invite what else young people may speak about, and it helps us communicate understanding and seek confirmation that we indeed do understand. Finally, by engaging the absent but implicit through double listening, and by listening to things other than words, we cultivate rich dialogical landscapes waiting to be explored for meaning and possibility.

## Highlights

### *From Active/Passive Listening to Listen-Ability*

| *Active Listening* | *Listen-Abilty* |
| --- | --- |
| Listening as discrete act | Listening as part of fluid relational practice |
| Listening without speaking | Speaking to listen |
| Listening only to voice of speaker | Attending to inner dialogue, listening to discourses, considering multiple perspectives |
| Listening to present and explicit | Listening for absent but implicit |
| Listening to single story | Double listening |

## Key Terms

1. **Absent but Implicit:** Michel White coined this term to illustrate how any expression used to relate an experience requires a distinction between that which is expressed and other experiences that have meaning. For example, to say that something is hot, we need an experience of cold. To say that we feel confused, we need an idea of clarity.
2. **Double Listening:** A listening practice advocated by Michael White that focuses on "hearing" and bringing forward both the absent but implicit as well as the present and explicit stories of any account.
3. **Inner Dialogue:** Within a dialogical/constructionist framework (Bakhtin 1981, 1984), the inner dialogue represents the "voices" of those people and ideas that influence and guide us in our relational engagements.
4. **Speaking to listen:** This blurs the binary of speaker/listener so that we approach conversations as a dialogical process of meaning making. When we're positioned to listen to young people in dialogue, much of what *we say* is said so that youth can say more.

## Discussion Questions

1. Write a user's guide titled, "How to Listen" with detailed instructions.
2. What barriers or challenges do you experience when trying to listen for the absent but implicit? Are there certain contexts or topics that make this more difficult? What ideas do you have that might help you double listen at those times?
3. How are you thinking about the relationship between listening and responding? What influences this?

4. In what ways do your listening practices change when you are listening from a social location with greater privilege than the social locations of the youth you're working with? What happens when you occupy a social location that holds less privilege than the youth?

## Notes

1 Queer theory is an elaboration of post-structural theory. Queer theory challenges the notion of essentialist identities and seeks to disrupt norms that impose limitations and specifications on people's identities and social practices. For a useful introduction, see Jagose (1996).
2 My use of the concept of inner dialogue is not from the tradition of individualism and essentialism that informs prevalent ideas of cognitive psychology that refer to "self-talk." Such ideas maintain that thoughts are produced "inside" our head or mind. My use of inner dialogue comes from the philosophy of language and dialogism that emphasize the social and relational nature of identity. Within this tradition, our inner dialogue is not the single voice of the "self;" rather, it is a polyphony of "voices" that influence us.
3 Their use of the term "client" reflects the context of psychotherapy that they were writing about.
4 Chapter 7 focuses in greater breadth and depth on kinds of questions and what they do in conversations.

# 6

# DO YA FEEL ME? UNDERSTANDING AND CONFIRMING MEANING

People understand me so poorly that they don't even understand my complaint about them not understanding me.

*Soren Kierkegaard*

There is a difference between a youth telling me something, and my under-standing it.

*Sam, a youth worker*

Chapter 5 focused on listening to understand and zeroing in on what matters to the young people we engage with. To further cultivate our listen-ability and capacity for meaningful engagement with youth, this chapter focuses on the spirit of relational work: understanding, compassion, and empathy. I'll break these down so that they're more than platitudes and become practices you embody when you show up in your work with youth.

## Be My Guest: Creating the Space for Understanding

Holding space is an aesthetic process—every detail matters.

*Eli, a youth worker*

I often hear youth workers talk about "creating a space" or "holding space" where young people feel like they can be themselves, participate openly, speak their mind, and do so liberated from the gaze of normative judgment and free from the threat of punitive action. This "space" can be both physical/literal and relational/metaphorical, and those two dimensions shape and influence one another in a reciprocal and generative way. Whereas a welcoming physical space holds meaning when the youth–adult relationships that occur within it are responsive to and honoring of young people, a physical space that *looks* inviting—perhaps cool and youth-centered—on the surface, ends up being a betrayal to young people if the relationships that happen in it fail to foster regard for the youth who frequent the space.

On the other hand, many youth ⸺ ⸺ ⸺ ⸺ ⸺ less than optimal circumstances—building ⸺ ⸺ windows through which to view the world ⸺ ⸺ urban squats littered with needles and used con ⸺, or rural fast food restaurants where everybody knows your name and your face—yet are able to create and hold a space through relational engagement, despite the challenging physical environment. These youth workers create space that allow young people to "bring all of themselves" (Tilsen, 2013, p. 3) to the conversation.

The extent to which you facilitate creation of such a space has a significant bearing on how young people show up. In turn, how young people show up directly relates to how well you will be able to "get" them. In this way, understanding becomes a relational accomplishment realized, in part, by the intentional way you create and hold space for youth work.

Think about it: have you ever felt understood by others when you've engaged with them while cautiously censoring yourself, feeling unwelcomed, or being concerned about your safety and their intentions? On the other hand, when have you felt most understood by others? What were the circumstances? I would imagine that this understanding was cultivated in the welcoming space of a relationship that allowed you to feel ⸺ ough to share meaningful things about your life.

What contributes to ⸺ ⸺ *itality* is one important part of making space for ⸺ ⸺ ⸺ y is about making others feel welcome and co⸺ ⸺ ⸺ ceiving others with kindness. It means that you are a gene⸺ ⸺ ⸺ nerous with your attention, interest, and warmth. You consider w⸺ ⸺ may be like for a young person in the situation and what may help them feel welcome and comfortable enough to show up in ways that allow you to get to know each other. It also means that you are a respectful *guest in the lives* of the young people you work with (Anderson, 2007) by honoring them as people and recognizing what they bring.

Ideally, hospitality is not only about what you do and say (for example, offer a beverage or snack, introduce yourself, ask what can make them comfortable, express your pleasure with seeing them, etc.); it can also be about what the physical space looks like. Is it a space that invites youth to settle in? Does it reflect the cultures and identities of the young people who will be in the space? What you do, what you say, and how the space looks are all expressions of welcoming the other.

Here are some other questions to consider: What is the name of the agency, program, or service? Is it something that resonates with young people and helps them feel good about participating? Do youth play a meaningful role in how the space looks? Sometimes adults have ideas about how places should look that end up communicating the opposite of hospitality to young people. At times, youth workers have to create a welcoming experience *despite* the physical environment or program policies. It's important to acknowledge programmatic and physical barriers to hospitality, such as non-inclusive language in paperwork. Not only can you work to change them, but you can also attend more earnestly to how you create hospitality relationally.

Another important consideration related to hospitality is *transparency*. Transparency involves demystifying what is going on by making the covert overt. When we're transparent, we share information about what will happen (or is likely to), what we're thinking and why, and how we've decided to go forward.

For example, when a group of young people arrive for the first day of camp, the counselors might let them know the general plans for the day and the reasoning that informs the schedule. This lets them know what to expect and it undoes the common practice of adults holding information. Or, if you are negotiating a conflict between two campers, transparency involves an explanation of why you've decided to have a conversation together and what the thinking is behind the questions you ask or suggestions you make. This makes your decisions and methods visible to youth. This visibility is a practice of accountability and contributes to the creation of a hospitable relational space that fosters understanding. Transparency is part of the fabric of narrative practice.

Transparency is different from *self-disclosure*. They do different things. Whereas transparency is about making the *process* of your work visible, self-disclosure involves sharing information about you and your personal life. What you disclose may have a connection to what you and the youth do together. For example, if the youth expresses excitement about going to the planetarium for the first time, and you tell them that the first time you went you found a $20 bill on the floor, it isn't about the structures, processes, or methods of your engagement: it's about you. Self-disclosure can be a routine part of an informal and friendly conversation (as in the above example). Or, it might be a way to convey understanding of a difficult situation or be part of a teachable moment (as in the example in the side bar on the next page).

Sometimes, self-disclosure is an indulgence that doesn't contribute to—and in fact may deter from—the engagement. We all do it. We may be preoccupied with something and we find a way to slip it into the conversation. Sometimes, in our effort to try to connect and convey understanding, we may share our feelings about what we see as a similar experience. The tricky part about this is that it can steer the conversation away from the young person and position them in a way that makes them feel responsible for taking care of us.

How can we work to prevent an unhelpful use of self-disclosure? Here are some questions about self-disclosure to ask yourself:

- Why am I sharing personal information? What do I want to accomplish and is there another way to accomplish it?

- What effects might it have on the conversation and the youth? Where does the focus go? Does it position the youth in a problematic way?
- Is this for me and about what will make me feel better, or is it for the youth and in their best interests?

---

## I Understand You…Let Me Tell You About Me

I was preparing a group of high school girls from a court-diversion program for a camping and rock climbing trip. None of them had ever left the city before. They were afraid of the trip and more afraid of the fear; in the worlds that they were from, acknowledgement of fear, self-doubt, and uncertainty was not an option. Their feelings were apparent by their sarcastic comments about the trip, their lack of enthusiasm, and the ways they would tease each other if anyone ever showed any evidence that they were remotely interested in the activities leading up to the trip. It was also pretty clear when one of the girls would announce daily, "this trip is bunk!"

I wanted to express my understanding that fear and doubt had taken hold of them. I needed a way to let them know I understood that didn't demand a confession or otherwise require that they submit themselves to an intimacy or vulnerability that they weren't seeking to enter. I wanted to honor their practices of protecting themselves, while also laying way for conversational paths to courage. I also hoped they might understand that these feelings didn't have to be the only story or the final story about them. I needed a story of transformation and possibility, one in which fear and doubt relinquished their starring roles as each of the girls took their place as the authoritative stars of their adventure-based story.

I shared with them the story of a backcountry winter trip in New England I had once taken. I described a group member who was always slow, afraid, in need of help, and generally lacking the skills and confidence of the other group members. I told them that this person was somewhat of a burden on the group. At the end of the story, I also told them that this person was me.

The impact on the group was profound. There was disbelief; they couldn't imagine me as the "group f-up." *What!? YOU were scared? No way!* They expressed concern about how the other group members responded: *Did they help you? Were they nice?* They desperately wanted to fill the gap between this story of fearful ineptitude and their perception of me as untouchable by doubt and incapable of failure. *How'd you stop being scared? When'd you become a wilderness boss?*

My story resonated with the group—it communicated understanding in a deep and sincere way. It let them know that I *got them.*

What do you think this self-disclosure made possible? How did it communicate understanding in a way that was hard to convey another way?

## Cultivating Compassion and Empathy

> If you're not curious about a youth, that says they don't matter. You can't have compassion and empathy about someone who doesn't matter, and if that's the case, get your shit together.
>
> *Emily, a youth worker*

I'll go out on a limb and make an assumption: If you do youth work, you believe that compassion and empathy are necessary for understanding and vital to doing solid youth work. I share that belief with you. Compassion and empathy are essential to understanding others. What are compassion and empathy and how do we *do* them?

*Compassion* is a global connection among people based on human experience. Compassion is a response to another's pain or difficulty that calls us to take action to relieve their suffering (Bein, 2008). When we show up with compassion, we are "present not only to possibilities but to pain" (Paré, 2013, p. 59).

What about empathy? When you experience empathy, someone else's experience strikes a chord with you in such a way that you have a sense of what it's like to be them—not how *you* would feel in that situation. When you show up with empathy, you *see The Other as Other*. You're not imagining yourself in that situation; you're imagining walking in their shoes. The relationship between understanding someone and experiencing compassion and empathy is important. Understanding generates from compassion, and as we come to have greater understanding of another, we come into more compassion and empathy.

What are some barriers to compassion and empathy? How can a constructionist approach help us show up compassionately and ready to walk in a youth's shoes so that we understand them?

Judgment (that is, a normative gaze), grand narratives (universal assumptions), and pressure to reach a conclusion can all hinder our ability to hold compassion. They are also all hallmarks of modernity, where professionals impose "expert" ideas from the outside in an effort to achieve goals they assume to be best. When we're caught up in these operations of modernity, frustration shows up, pushing compassion aside, and compromises our capacity to understand another. A constructionist stance positions us to consider multiple perspectives and question the power relations inherent in normative assumptions that jeopardize our capacity to understand.

When I experience this frustration, I try to *slow down, back up, and look around*. I slow down my rush to get to a solution or resolution, I back up to get alongside the youth in the conversation instead of out ahead of them, and I look around to consider the context of the young person's world to generate a richer understanding. I ask myself: *What do I need to understand about their experience, from their perspective, to have compassion for them?* Greater understanding leads to compassion, and compassion makes room for greater understanding.

Another barrier to compassion, empathy, and understanding involves the challenge to get outside of our own worldview and personal experience. This is especially true when we occupy privileged social locations. Our unearned privileges and the centering of our worldview is not visible to us—that's part of privilege (Johnson, 2006). This invisibility of systemic privilege operates as a barrier to the understanding of and compassion for others who do not share those privileges.

For example, as a white person I will never know what it means to be a person of color in the United States, and as a cisgender person I will never understand how it feels to be transgender. The positioning practices and post-structural analysis of power explored in Part I are resources that can help us account for our privilege and the ways power operates through systems of privilege. Ultimately, to understand others, we must *believe them*. This can present a challenge: in order to believe that others have different experiences than we do, we must undo the centrality and universality of our experiences. We must acknowledge that there are multiple truths and ways people experience the world.

The following questions can help move us closer to understanding how others experience the world. Each of these questions invite you to reflect on your experience when socially located with privilege. The last two questions in each grouping ask you about situations directly related to youth work. Consider the questions that are relevant to the social locations you occupy.

1.  How does your experience as a white person differ from the experience of a person of color in:
    - Getting credit approved?
    - Passing police on the street?
    - Asking a supervisor for help?
    - Meeting with a youth worker you have racial affinity with?
    - Being the youth worker for a youth of color?
2.  How does your experience as a heterosexual person differ from the experience of a queer person in:
    - Expressing affection, love, or comfort in public?
    - Talking about your dating life with coworkers?
    - Consuming popular culture images and music?
    - Seeking relationship counseling?
    - Being the relationship counselor for a queer youth?
3.  How does your experience as a non-Indigenous person differ from the experience of an Indigenous person in:
    - Discussing your child's educational needs with their school?
    - Reading a book or seeing a film about the history of the country in which you live?
    - Experiencing cultural appropriation?
    - Working with a grief counselor?
    - Being the grief counselor for an indigenous youth?
4.  How does your experience as a cisgender person differ from the experience of a transgender or gender nonconforming person in:
    - Filling out forms for school, the government, jobs, etc.?
    - Using the bathroom?

- Crossing international borders?
- Participating in your school's athletics program?
- Coaching a trans or gender nonconforming youth in a school athletics program?

5. How does your experience as a non-disabled person differ from the experience of a person with a disability in:
   - Being able to move easily in your work or educational spaces?
   - How people interpret expressions of anger or frustration?
   - Being seen as competent and credible in your job?
   - Seeking advocacy within the healthcare system?
   - Being the healthcare advocate for a youth with a disability?

6. How does your experience as a Christian differ from the experience of a person from a different spiritual tradition in:
   - Making plans around holidays?
   - Taking time off of school or work for religious observances?
   - How you feel about "casual" comments like, "Merry Christmas," "Have a good Easter," or "God bless you"?
   - Finding spiritually specific activities and services?
   - Incorporating youths' spiritual traditions into your youth work practice?

7. How does your experience as a financially stable person differ from the experience of an economically marginalized person in:
   - Dressing appropriately for the winter or for a job interview?
   - Being able to take "mental health days" from work?
   - Participating in social and recreational activities with coworkers?
   - Being available to attend meetings and appointments for your child during work hours?
   - Accommodating youths' schedules and ability to pay for activities and services?

8. How might your experience as a man differ from the experience of a women in:
   - Traveling alone?
   - Being seen as knowledgeable or credible?
   - Dressing "down" without judgment of others?
   - Seeing a male service provider?
   - Being a male's youth worker?

9. How might your experience as a person born in the United States differ from the experience of a person from another country in:
   - Seeking care in an ER?
   - Traveling by plane?
   - Saying "I don't understand, please repeat that..."?
   - Complaining to a program manager about your children's youth worker?
   - Being the youth worker parents complain about to a program manager?

   *(Adapted from the Dulwich Centre Privilege Project)*[1]

Reflecting on how privilege influences us is one aspect of considering someone else's experience in order to cultivate understanding. Even when we share social locations or identity markers with others, we must constantly ask ourselves: *What do I need to understand about how their particular experience is different from mine in order to really understand?* And, *what assumptions am I making that keep me from understanding?* Coming to an understanding is a constant negotiation of meaning. This requires a committed effort to expose and resist assumptions that lead us too quickly to be too certain about who others are and what matters to them.

---

### Intersectionality

These questions about privilege each focused on one dimension of identity. However, our identities are multiple and we live at the intersections of these multiplicities. Our experience of privilege or marginalization is contextual. After you've had some time with these questions, go back through the questions and step into a variety of intersections. For example, if you are white and queer, consider how your world differs from that of a queer person of color. If you're an American-born, black Christian, think about how your experiences differ from a Somali Muslim refugee.

What are some things that are new for you to consider? Are you experiencing compassion or empathy in ways that you previously hadn't? How might reflecting on your privilege help you cultivate greater understanding for others?

---

### Experience-Near Conversations: Talking in Their Terms

> I want to use their language while making connections to make new language or a new idea available to them, while keeping it true to their meaning.
>
> *Angela, a youth worker*

What are some conversational practices that steer us away from assumptions and move toward understanding? Geertz's (1976) idea of *experience-near description* is useful toward these ends.

Experience-near descriptions use personal, particular, non-structuralist language and understandings, while *experience-distant descriptions* rely on global, structuralist meanings (White, 2005) that often include professional jargon. Experience-near descriptions include the words used by the person to tell their story, and/or other language that resonates with them. They also rely on the meanings and understanding that the person holds. This evokes a feeling of being understood, whereas experience-distant descriptions fail to do so. Using experience-near descriptions is an accountability practice that helps us prevent creeping assumptions and the imposition of adult/expert knowledge.

For example, I was in a consultation with some school-based youth workers who offer classroom support, tutoring, and social activities for middle schoolers.

When describing the students, they would often use language that reflected adultist and professionalized understandings of the students. Phrases such as, "he has anger management issues," or "she engages in attention-seeking behaviors when experiencing stressful situations" were commonplace. Other descriptions frequently used included, "triggered," "depressed," and "easily redirected." All of these ways of languaging youths' practices and social acts reflect universalized, professionalized terms and concepts. In other words, they are likely (I say likely, because it's certainly possible that some youth might use them to describe themselves) experience-distant descriptions.

---

### #FergusonSyllabus Question

How can "experience-near" descriptions demonstrate appreciation for and understanding of youths' worlds? How do "experience-distant" descriptions reproduce expert/adultist discourses and practices of colonization?

---

I asked the youth workers how the students would describe each of the situations that the youth workers had discussed. The difference between the universal descriptions offered by the youth workers, and the more particular ways that they imagined each young person would recount their own experiences were striking. For example, one youth worker acknowledged that while "depressed" was the word she used to describe a youth, this young person would often talk about "not feeling right and not being myself." We talked about what the team had come to know about this student, what mattered to her, and what some of the context was surrounding her current experiences. We then practiced generating some alternative experience-near descriptions, such as, "The changes at home have you not feeling right and like you're not yourself, and this is making school feel really hard to do, is that right?"

As another example, several youth workers said that the student they had described as having "anger management issues" would describe herself as "feeling mad about the stupid things we have to do." This is the experience-near description they came up with: "There's all kinds of stupid things you're made to do at school that don't make any sense, you're feeling mad about them, and you're not wanting to put up with them, am I getting that right?"

Both of these examples illustrate that experience-near descriptions involve:

- Using some of the young person's own words;
- Some paraphrasing, that is, using words that are close to, but not precisely the same as, those used by the youth. Paraphrasing gets at the intended meaning and focuses on what matters to and resonates with the youth;
- Deliberate avoidance of expert/professional language and meanings.

You will also notice that these examples included a *confirmation of meaning* (e.g. "did I get that right?"). This is not an aspect of experience-near descriptions, per se; rather, it is a conversational practice that works in concert with experience-near descriptions. Seeking confirmation by asking a question in this way lets the young person know that you are holding your understanding lightly and without certainty, and that you will defer to them to approve or adjust the understanding you've come to. Confirming meaning and asking for the young person's feedback on your rendering of their description is a practice that reflects an ethic of care and collaborative construction of meaning.

Sticking with experience-near descriptions is an act of accountability as it keeps us from interpreting and imposing expert-driven meanings. We avoid the certainty and assumptions inherent in expert edicts, thus opening space for connection, meaning making, and a richer understanding of youth on their terms.

Something else stood out to the youth workers in this consultation: they noticed that they were able to detail how *some* of their students would discuss *some* of their experiences, but not all. They took this as an indication that they hadn't yet come to hold rich understandings of all their students. This led to their decision to practice using experience-near descriptions, check themselves when they slipped into "expert-ese" (a term one of them coined to describe professional jargon), and check with their students to see if they were getting them. They made extra efforts to do so with the young people for whom they couldn't generate an experience-near description. When we are unable to render an experience-near description—that is, use the language the youth uses and convey the meaning they have—we are not understanding as fully as we can. We're not getting them on their terms.

Understanding the young people we work with, cultivating compassion and empathy, and generating rich experience-near descriptions means that we've gotten to know them on their terms, in their terms. I ask myself, "*how would this young person describe their experience?*" not as a way to speak *for* them. On the contrary, I ask myself this question to hold myself accountable. If I can't approximate an answer that they would endorse, I certainly shouldn't jump into an experience-distant rendering loaded with adultist and professionalized language and colored with my own assumptions.

Connecting understanding to compassion and empathy is important when we're engaging with young people around difficult experiences. What about understanding when youth are trying to express joy, contentment, or excitement? How do we make sure we get them when there's good stuff? Seeking to understand what matters to a young person—whether it *seems* like a big deal (going to their first concert in a big venue) or mundane (having tacos for dinner)—is always about suspending our assumptions, assessments, and worldview in order to see things from their perspective. The same conversational practices described above are useful when you're working to understand and really *get* the good stuff that matters to youth, too.

## Summary

How do we generate experience-near descriptions and negotiate understanding? This is a quintessential question for constructionists. Embracing multiple perspectives; accounting for operations of power in discourse, our social locations, and institutional structures; suspending the need for agreement, resolution, or consensus; and creating space that invites difference and variety all serve as ethical aspirations to foster understanding. Taking these from aspirational to operational is the challenge, in part because in doing so, we run the risk of mechanizing the relational. Understanding is a relational process.

As such, it's important to approach understanding as an ongoing social practice of negotiating and making meaning. Ultimately, *getting* someone else—whether it's about what is awesome and important, or it's something that's awful and important, and everything in between—is about avoiding conclusions, staying curious, and *asking*. The next chapter takes up the matter of curiosity and the art of asking questions.

## Highlights

| Achieving Understanding | Barriers to Understanding |
| --- | --- |
| Hospitality: physical space and relational space | Unwelcoming, adult-centered |
| Transparency and self-disclosure | Opaque process/methods and one-way exchange |
| Compassion and empathy | Grand narratives, "expert" knowledge, normative judgment |
| Decenter worldview and expose/account for privilege | Universal worldview and unexamined privilege |
| Experience-near descriptions | Experience-distant descriptions |
| Seek confirmation of meaning/ understanding | Assume meaning and achievement of understanding |

## Key Terms

1. **Compassion:** Compassion is our response to the suffering or struggles of others that compels us to take action on their behalf.
2. **Confirmation of meaning:** Confirmation of meaning is a practice of accountability and negotiation of meaning in which you check in to see if you're understanding the person(s) you're talking with.
3. **Empathy:** Empathy refers to the sense of and ability to feel what someone else feels and to "walk in their shoes." It does not mean that you envision how *you* would feel in the same situation; rather empathy requires that you understand how the other feels.

4.  **Experience-near description:** Experience-near descriptions rely on the personal and particular words used, meaning made, and understanding held by the person whose experience is described. This is in contrast to an **experience-distant description,** which imposes expert or professional language and understandings, often which reflect universal rather than local knowledge.

5.  **Hospitality:** Hospitality refers to things you do and say to help others feel welcome and comfortable. It involves receiving others with kindness and is reflected in the places, programs, and practices of youth work.

6.  **Self-disclosure:** Self-disclosure involves sharing information about your personal life, or things that otherwise are not necessarily connected to the process of and engagement in youth work activities.

7.  **Transparency:** Transparency involves demystifying what is going on by making the covert overt. This means that we are sharing the processes, methods, intentions, and thinking involved with what we are doing together with youth, giving them a "behind the scenes" view.

## Discussion Questions

1.  Have you ever said or heard another youth worker say, "hold space" or "create space?" What has been your understanding of this? What ideas do you have about how to partner with young people in the creation of meaningful conversational spaces?

2.  What experiences have you had with experience-distant descriptions, where someone else has used language that failed to resonate with you or convey understanding? What was that like for you? What effect did it have on the relationship?

3.  When have you had difficulty offering an experience-near description of someone? What got in the way? What helps you remove those barriers?

4.  Discuss your thoughts about transparency and self-disclosure. How do you see yourself engaging in these? What questions or hesitations do you have?

## Note

1 The Dulwich Centre in Adelaide, AU first offered a series of reflection questions about privilege on their website in 2004. Over the years, I have adapted the questions for different contexts. You can read about the original project at: dulwichcentre. com.au/a-continuing-invitation-to-narrative-practitioners-to-address-privilege-and-dominance/.

# 7

# I'M NOT TELLING, I'M ASKING

## The Art and Craft of Curiosity

Always the beautiful answer who asks a more beautiful question.

*E. E. Cummings*

In order to be curious, you have to be creative.

*Eli, a youth worker*

Chapters 4, 5, and 6 covered many aspects of conversational practice that reflect a praxis of knowing, doing, and being (J. White, 2007). These include the shift from monologue to dialogue, listening for the absent but implicit, and cultivating understanding and offering experience-near descriptions. Throughout the discussions, examples, and vignettes in these chapters, you undoubtedly noticed that questions are a big part of the conversational practice. Many of the questions in the vignettes may not have been what you expected!

Indeed, constructionist-informed practices don't skimp on questions. In fact, questions are the main course of a narrative conversation. This chapter will present a practice of respectful and generative curiosity in which questions give conversations shape and open pathways to all kinds of possibilities.

## Why Curiosity? On Refusing Certainty and Resisting Conclusions

Earnest questions disengage adultist power dynamics and help me come from a place of not-knowing instead of knowing-better than.

*Eli, a youth worker*

We live in a culture where curiosity seems to be at a fevered pitch: we frenetically click sensational headlines (but rarely read full articles), we google everything from historical dates to hysterical videos, and we feed an insatiable interest in naughty celebrities and adorable kittens. Curiosity may not kill us, but the whiplash we get from bouncing from every compelling thing that comes our way just might give us a major pain in the neck. *That* is *not* the kind of curiosity this chapter is about.

What does curiosity look like in a narrative approach to youth work? Recall some of the central concepts and values of constructionist philosophy and post structural theory such as: rejection of universal truths and grand narratives, emphasis on understanding rather than agreement, embrace of multiple perspectives and realities, questioning assumptions, and disrupting dominating discourses. These all require the kind of curiosity that allows us *to wonder* beyond what we know…or think we know. This curiosity is hungry to understand, welcomes surprises, and avoids self-righteous devotion to any truths that would prevent other truths from emerging.

When we approach young people with a genuine curiosity to understand them free from normative judgment, we embody our relational ethics. Furthermore, cultivating curiosity allows us to creatively and actively deconstruct power operations and dominating discourses—it takes an acute degree of inquisitiveness to unravel the layers of invisible assumptions embedded in systems of power. This curiosity also implies a refusal to accept that what we see is all we get; that is, we refuse to accept that there isn't more to know, or more ways to know. This is critical in youth work. When we assume that we know, "we lose the curiosity necessary to inquire about alternative identities and acts of resistance" (Tilsen, 2013, p. 14)—two things at the heart of work with young people. We also participate in conventional adultist power relations by imposing meaning and disregarding youth's perspectives.

How do we show up with curiosity? Here are a few principles that help us engage with curiosity:

- *Suspend our assumptions.* This is a central premise of constructionist philosophy that we've covered at length. In order to inquire about something different and enter another's world, we have to acknowledge what makes up our world (Madsen & Gillespie, 2014).
- *Engage with wonder.* According to the Merriam-Webster dictionary, one definition of *wonder* is: "rapt attention or astonishment at something awesomely mysterious or new to one's experience." *That's* the kind of curiosity I try to show up with. Conversations abundant with wonder manifest at the intersection of curiosity, imagination, and love of young people and youth work.
- *Partner with youth as "co-researchers."* Epston (1998, 1999) describes *co-research* as a partnership in which both youth worker and young person engage in curiosity together in order to "research" new possibilities and consider novel alternatives.
- *Assume a "not-knowing" approach.* Anderson and Goolishian's (1988) notion of "not-knowing" refers to a philosophical stance that positions the youth

worker to stay open to a variety of meanings and engage with genuine curiosity. This stance prevents us from being too quick to know young people's experience or what they mean when they talk. "Not knowing" does *not* imply that youth workers have no knowledge, skills, preferences, biases, etc. It does mean we stay curiously engaged as we negotiate understanding and resist assumptions and conclusions.

- *Cultivate your question-asking craft.* Curiosity informs good questions, good questions feed imagination, imagination inspires conversation, and inspired conversation invites curiosity. I approach question-asking as a craft that requires intentional, deliberate practice[1] in order to be an effective question asker.

In preparation for a dive into the kinds of questions we can ask, not to mention how to weave the asking into a conversation, let's first consider the praxis relationship between constructionist and post-structural theories and the practice of using questions in a narrative approach to youth work.

## Why Questions? Connecting Practice to Theory, Politics, and Ethics

> Questions give youth a chance to comment on how other people story their lives.
>
> *Emily, a youth worker*

As discussed in Part I, social construction and post-structural theory champion a stance of unhinging universal assumptions and engaging skepticism in regard to taken-for-granted operations of power. Questioning ideas that usually go unquestioned and avoiding certainty creates openings for new, often novel, alternatives. Furthermore, when we challenge dominating power relations by calling into question the assumptions embedded within them, we are embodying relational responsibility and an ethic of care. In short, a question-driven practice reflects the theoretical, philosophical, and ethical stances advanced in this book. I don't mean just *any* questions—we'll zero in on types of questions that emerge from the spirit of meaningful and respectful curiosity later in the chapter.

First, I'm going to turn to praxis and consider the relationship between the central concepts we've already covered and the use of questions in youth work practice. I'll break these down so that you can refer back to the chapter that featured each idea.

*How does a question-driven practice reflect a constructionist stance? Ideas from Chapter 1:*

1.  Language is productive—it does things, it doesn't simply describe things. As we move from a visual to a textual metaphor, where our interest moves from things to stories, our talk also shifts from monologue to dialogue. Questions

help facilitate dialogue because *questions help move conversations.* Think about the difference between statements and questions. What do statements do and what do questions do? Of course, context matters, but generally, statements communicate information and do not invite a response outside of, perhaps, confirmation (Paré, 2013). On the other hand, an interesting question asked at the right moment builds generative dialogue and ensures that "meaning is on the move" (McNamee, personal communication, 2010).

2. Social construction embraces a nonessentialist notion of identity and is interested in how people shape their identities in relationship to their social world. Asking questions gives young people space to speak their identities into the world in meaningful and productive ways. Question-asking also serves to expose and challenge essentialist limitations and specifications often imposed on young people's identities. This helps youth bring forward and further their understandings of how their identities are in relationship with cultural discourses.

*How does a question-driven practice reflect attention to power? Ideas from Chapter 2:*

1. One way to attend to and account for power is to take care in how we position ourselves relationally with young people. Assuming a decentered but influential position helps us account for power operations, and one of the most effective ways to take this position is by asking questions rather than making statements. Again, think about the difference between statements and questions. Whose ideas are central in a statement? When we ask respectfully curious questions, we decenter our power. As you will see, I am interested in asking questions that invite young people's knowledges and preferences and that position them to exercise authority in their lives.

2. A primary goal of a post-structural analysis of power is to deconstruct and challenge prevailing discourses. This includes calling into question the power of totalizing single-story accounts of youth identity and the assumption that power operates only in one direction. By definition, deconstruction of prevailing discourses—itself a challenge to the power inherent in them—is an active process of questioning. Partnering with young people in this deconstructive process is a practice of resistance, a challenge to the specifications of power relations typical in adult-youth relationships. When we do more telling than asking, we participate in the power relations we seek to disrupt.

*How does a question-driven practice reflect an ethic of care and relational responsibility? Ideas from Chapter 3:*

1. The consideration of ethics is inseparable from that of power; they go hand in hand. When we attend to power and positioning as described before, we are practicing accountability, which is an ethical matter. Thus, we

embody an ethic of care when we use questions that center youth knowledge and author-ity and decenter adult and professional expertise. As stated in Chapter 3, these are not only technical or practice decisions, these are ethical decisions as well.

2. An important facet of relational responsibility entails a shift from rules to relationships. One way to realize this shift is to embrace the idea of *ethics as questions* (Freedman & Combs, 1996). This means we are asking questions of ourselves about our practice and the effects of it. We engage critically and question assumptions embedded in our practice in order to deconstruct and challenge operations of power and show up in more accountable ways with youth.

Having made these connections between the conceptual foundations presented in Part I and a question-driven practice, I suggest that you now look back at some of the vignettes and examples presented in previous chapters. Can you see the connection between theory and the practice of question-asking? How do the questions asked reflect the tenets of social construction and post-structural theory?

---

## Questioning as Act of Resistance

When I was in Amsterdam, I visited the Dutch Resistance Museum. This museum houses a rich collection of artifacts that documents the Dutch resistance to the Nazi occupation of the Netherlands during World War II. As a Jew, I had a powerful and provocative experience. The collection includes radio clips, doctor's notes, photos of hiding places, resistance newspapers, and much, much more. As you enter the exhibit, you see a quote on the wall from Remco Campert (a Dutch author and poet whose father died in a Nazi concentration camp): *"Asking yourself a question, that's how resistance begins. And then ask that very question to someone else."*

This quote resonated deeply with me. It captured for me the core of deconstruction: questioning the assumptions that uphold the status quo. It also spoke to the post-structural nerd in me as I read it as an example of not only deconstruction, but also as an example of the multi-directionality of power (recall the Foucault quote in Chapter 2, "where there's power there's resistance"). And, it demonstrates the relational and productive qualities of questions: questions *do* things, and they do them when we're in relationship with others.

Asking certain questions of particular discourses, structures, or institutions, is itself an act of resistance. What are some discourses you have questioned in your life as an act of resistance? How did you question them? Who would you like to join you in your questioning?

## What Kinds of Questions Are We Talking About?
## Questions That Do Different Things

> Questions define your intention in the relationship.
>
> *Angela, a youth worker*

*DISCLAIMER*: There are so many different kinds of questions and so many ways to categorize them. There are books written about questions. In this section, of this chapter, of this book, my intentions are: (1) to provide examples of some of the kinds of questions that are likely to be most helpful for you and that reflect the concepts presented in this book, (2) illuminate the relationship between the questions and the conceptual resources outlined in this book, and (3) provide examples of their use in conversations with youth.

As with all things that are rich and complex, there is more out there than you will find in here. And, as with all things that you want to develop a deep understanding of and cultivate sophisticated skills in, question-asking demands ongoing attention and commitment.

Actually, this disclaimer applies to all the concepts and practices in this book; there is much more to know about these ideas. Why did I write a disclaimer for this section? I especially want to underscore that having a dialogical question-driven practice isn't simply a matter of picking the right ingredients and throwing a conversation together, or, in regard to questions, choosing a question from a buffet and dropping it in the midst of a conversation. Throughout this book, I have run the risk of reducing complex interconnected concepts and practices to tinker toy parts that you can pick up and snap together (leaving some behind if they're uninteresting to you or seem hard to work with) without regard for the complexities of their interrelatedness. This feels especially true when I make a list of "types of questions."

Adhering to Aristotle's maxim, *the whole is greater than the sum of its parts* is a nonnegotiable at this point, one which I hope serves as a gentle nudge to

---

### #FergusonSyllabus Question

Making spaces for youth to "have a say" in their lives and communities is often fundamental to youth work. As youth workers, shifting from making statements to asking questions can be a powerful path to youth agency.

How can we use a relational process of thoughtful inquiry based on curiosity and wonder as a foundation for liberatory youth work with young people living on the margins of society? What would be important and interesting to inquire about?

remember praxis. In the spirit of praxis, and as an entry point to this section on questions, I will ask you to reflect on the following question as you consider each of the following examples: *What concepts from social construction and post-structural theory does this question reflect?* You may prefer to think of this question as: *How is this question informed by social construction and post-structural theory?*

## A World of Questions: Beyond "Open" and "Closed"

> A so-called closed question can invite a response that opens lots of possibilities.
>
> *Emily, a youth worker*

We've all heard it before: *Ask open questions, don't ask closed questions.* It's way past time to retire that overly simplistic notion and enter a world of questions that offers so much more nuance and complexity. Not only are there more descriptive and specific ways of grouping questions, but there really is no such thing as a completely open or a completely closed question.[2] Finally, I am cautious about evaluating or valuing a question based on the kind of question it is if it's *disembodied from a conversation* and the people engaged in it. All questions can be meaningful, even ones that elicit a "yes" or "no" response—it depends on the context and what you're hoping the question will do, and what significance the response holds.

### Questions that Make Stories

> I want to know about you, your values, your wants, not just you in your trauma and moments that other people have defined as important to know. Those don't have to be the defining moments. I ask questions that allow youth to tell the story they want.
>
> *Angela, a youth worker*

Who, what, where, why, when, and how. These are the questions I remember my first-grade teacher, Mrs. Beasley at Kenwood Elementary School in Minneapolis, encouraging us to think about when we were learning to write a story. In constructionist-informed youth work, we listen to stories (some which may be inaudible to the person speaking it) and at times, we contribute to the re-authoring of stories. Re-authoring is, as discussed in previous chapters, a dialogical process of transformation, one which brings forward identities previously unknown or unavailable to young people. Those same questions that Mrs. Beasley taught me to ask almost 50 years ago still work, and you will see them put to use in various forms in the questions that follow. These are the questions that help us tell stories.

The following categories are definitely not exhaustive and certainly not discrete—questions can do more than one thing. The types of questions listed as follows all play a part in a young person's claim on their storytelling rights. These questions are also central to transformative conversations that help youth re-author totalizing identities. Effective, meaningful questions point to conversational pathways of possibility.

1. **Deconstructive questions:** These questions challenge the assumptions and truth claims embedded within prevailing discourses and institutions by exposing contextual contingencies that go unacknowledged and unquestioned. Deconstruction denaturalizes "taken-for-granteds." Deconstruction situates youth's experiences in discourse and helps them resist the burden of individualism and privatization of social problems.
   - What unspoken rules are there on the team about playing when hurt?
   - Have you heard of the same rules on the girls' hockey team as these rules on the boys' team?
   - Who enforces these unspoken rules about how to be a man's man? What are the penalties for breaking a rule? What are the costs of following them?

2. **Meaning making questions:** These questions invite reflection on ideas, actions, preferences, and values in order to assign significance (meaning) to them. Giving meaning helps connect young people to new possibilities for identity conclusions and ways of doing and being in the world.
   - What is it about gardening that you love so much?
   - How did gardening make its way into your heart even though you first thought it was stupid?
   - Now that gardening is not stupid, how does it make sense to you that you actually like it? How does it "fit" with your other interests and what's important to you?

3. **Re-authoring questions:** These questions are most directly connected to identity as they invite youth to ascribe meaning to and claim ideas, actions, preferences, and values that uphold a preferred identity. They bring forward unique outcomes and lead to the development of alternative stories.
   - What did you have to know and what skills did you have to have to get an interview?
   - When you found out that your old probation officer (P.O.) was part of the interview team, did you remind yourself of anything in particular so that you wouldn't fall into who he expected you to be?
   - How would you describe who your old P.O. thought he knew and who he actually got to meet in the interview?
   - When would you say you started to show up as this "new and improved" version of yourself?

4. **Consultative questions:** These questions access and validate youth expertise, enlisting young people as experts on their own lives. Consultative

questions promote collaboration between youth worker and young person, and thicken youths' stories of preferred identity.

- What suggestions do you have for other youth who want to get their school to have discussions about racism?
- What are some of the challenges or barriers you'd tell others to look out for?
- How would you describe what you need to know and the skills you need to have to address this issue at a school?
- What advice would you give to other students of color about working with white school administrators?

5. **Inoculation questions:** These questions reinforce any changes that a youth has made and mobilize their determination to meet future challenges. Inoculation questions also help take inventory of skills, knowledges, and resources the young person has developed.
   - If you were going to go back and let drugs take over your life again, what would you have to do, or not do, to let drugs do that?
   - Where would be some of the best places for you to hang out if you wanted drugs to pick you up?
   - Who would drugs want you to ignore so that they could get you back?
   - What do you know now, that you didn't before, that drugs would want you to forget?

6. **Scaling questions:** These questions help youth articulate more specific and concrete descriptions of their experiences if they are having a hard time doing so. Scaling questions also encourage recognition that things aren't "all or nothing" and can make visible small but significant changes.
   - If 1 means, "camp is the worst, I'm so homesick, get me out of here now" and 10 means, "camp is most awesome and I'm never going to leave," where are you now?
   - When has it been higher? Lower?
   - What would (their number +1) look like or feel like? What would be happening?
   - What's keeping it from being (their number -1)? What are you doing to keep it from being lower? Who else is helping it from going lower?

7. **Coping questions:** These questions help youth claim what they are doing on their own behalf during difficult situations or when hopelessness is present. Coping questions open doors to alternative stories and encourage meaning making.
   - What does it take for you to keep filling out housing applications after so many dead-ends?
   - How do you keep the frustration from being even worse than it is?
   - What would it take for you to keep doing what you've been doing?
   - Where did you learn to keep at it like this? Who inspired you?

8. **Exceptions or unique outcomes questions:** These questions invite youth to notice and claim times when they've done (or thought or imagined)

something that contradicts a dominating problem narrative about them. Exceptions and unique outcomes questions help young people resist totalizing accounts of their identities and open paths to alternative stories.

- Before organizing this protest, have there ever been times where you imagined feeling even a little bit satisfied with how you did something?
- Does feeling proud about organizing so many youth for the protest suggest that it's a lie that you never feel content with what you can do?
- What story about yourself did you have to resist so you'd feel okay with your organizing efforts? Is this why you're feeling proud about it?
- What would you like to come from this new experience of feeling okay and proud about what you do?

9. **Time traveling questions:** These questions invite young people to reflect on changes or future possible changes by using the temporal dimension as a frame of reference. Time traveling questions make visible small but significant changes that have happened, and make possible changes that are yet to happen.

- Six months ago, what would have happened if you had walked into a fight in the drop-in center?
- When was the turning point that took you from joining fights to stopping fights?
- If someone had told you six months ago that you'd be breaking up fights, not picking up fights, what would you have said?
- What do you think you might be doing six months from now that today seems unbelievable?

10. **Multiple perspectives questions:** These questions ask youth to reflect on something in their life through the eyes of an important figure.[3] Inviting perspectives from those with whom young people are in meaningful relationships makes visible skills, knowledges, and exceptions that the young person may not see on their own.

- If you could see yourself through your best friend's eyes, what would you notice about how you are a friend that you don't see when you look through your own eyes?
- What would your dog say are your best relationship skills?
- Who in your life wouldn't be surprised that it matters to you how you treat others?
- You said that the sorting hat put you in Hufflepuff, the house known for loyalty, hard work, and justice. If you went to Hogwarts without wearing your colors, what would people notice that would let them know what house you belong to?

Keeping these examples in mind, how do you describe the way curiosity is working? How would you describe the kind of curiosity these questions carry? What else is "inside" these questions? What are these questions doing?

Sometimes, when you read a series of questions that are either plucked out of a conversation, or are teaching examples (as before), they can feel like an inquisition or an incredibly lopsided and aloof one-way interview. It's also important to remember that questions are not mere techniques or mechanical maneuvers; when done well, they carry the *relational responsiveness* and reflect the *listen-ability* previously discussed. Questions that emerge from the conversation and resonate with youth *show that you are engaged*. You may recall from Chapter 5 the idea of *speaking to listen*. Questions are the most important iteration of this, as they specifically invite young people to say more.

It's pretty common that, when we're learning anything new, things can feel kind of clunky. The more you immerse yourself in a constructionist stance and engage reflexively in praxis *while practicing questions* (and by practice, I don't mean only while in conversation with youth; I mean *practice*, as in review over and over), the more fluid you will become in the art and craft of curiosity.

---

### Question Do's and Don'ts

- Do not ask questions to collect information for the purpose of formulating a theory about youth, rendering a professional edict, or conjuring an interpretation.
- Do not ask questions to which you have (or *think* you have) the answer.
- Do not ask questions that privatize social problems and disregard context and power operations.
- Do not ask questions that feature professional jargon or other language that doesn't reflect and resonate with youth.
- Do ask questions that emerge from the conversation you are having.
- Do ask questions that have developed from and reflect your sincere curiosity.
- Do ask questions intended to generate new ideas, induce imaginary circumstances, invite confusion in the place of certainty, and provoke previously unthought of possibilities.
- Do ask questions infused with wonder.
- Do ask questions that bring forward and center youth knowledge and skills.
- Do ask questions that work to contextualize youth experience and situate it in relation to cultural discourses and systems of dominance.
- Do ask questions that use and reflect the language and aesthetic of youth.

### Still More Kinds of Questions: Response-Based Practice

I focus on both their struggles and their goals.

*Mickella, a youth worker*

*Response-based practice* and response-based questions (Coates & Wade, 2007; Richardson, 2015; Wade, 1997; M. White, 2007) are another useful way to categorize questions. These questions invite young people to center their agency and bring forward what matters to them in response to oppression. Response-based questions are different from *effects* questions; effects questions focus on what happens to people, while response questions are about what people do in response to what happens.

Response-based practice was originally conceptualized as an alternative practice with people who have experienced violence. The essential idea is that conventional language practices, including the questions we ask people in relationship-based services, have historically focused on effects—what happens to people.

For example, we might ask a youth, *"how do you feel about the other youth making transphobic comments?"* or, *"how is your boyfriend cheating on you affecting you now?"* Effects questions cast people as passive victims and assume that all effects are negative results of what happened. This leads to a single story that ignores or erases the acts of resistance that people engage in. Focusing on effects also tends to obscure context and institutionalized systems of oppression, thus contributing to the privatization of social problems. Indeed, the language of effects obfuscates the person(s) or system that inflict the harm (Wade, 1997) and conflates what happens to a person with their identity. In fact, it can *become* their identity.

Let's see how this works in the example below.

*Andy bullied Sahra.*
*Sahra was bullied by Andy.*
*Sahra was bullied.*
*Sahra is a victim of bullying.*

In the above example, Sahra has a totalizing identity imposed on her, while Andy and his actions disappear. Historically, conversations influenced by these language practices inquire only into the effects of Sahra's experience, such as fear, anger, or shame. These conversations fail to ask about Sahra's actions in response to bullying and the meanings she assigns to her responses.

Furthermore, it's typically assumed that the effect of, for example, fear is only a negative product of bullying, and not a meaningful response that points to what matters to Sahra. A fundamental assumption of response-based practice is that collapsing these problems onto individuals and their identities is politically and ethically problematic, as is the exclusive focus on negative effects. Young people exist in the social world and their struggles are in the social world. Ethical youth work practice demands that we name the social practices and structures of oppression that impact youth and our relationships with them. This is a praxis point where the principles of relational responsibility meet up with conversational practice.

Alternatively, response based practices put into action the Foucauldian tenet of power operations mentioned in Chapter 2: *where there's power there's resistance*. This idea reflects another assumption of response-based practice: people always respond to oppressive or traumatic events in their lives. Their responses are expressions of what matters to them, reflecting their values, intentions, hopes, and preferred ways of being in the world. Asking about youth's response to oppressive effects of power brings forward their stories of resistance. This involves a shift in language from:

- victim to agent;
- effects to response;
- single story to multiple stories;
- professional knowledge to local/cultural knowledge (storytelling rights);
- individual to relational/contextual.

What does this look like in practice? For example, we may ask, "what did you do when you heard the others making transphobic comments?" or, "what does the sadness you feel about your boyfriend cheating on you say about the importance of that relationship?" Both questions position the youth as an active agent in their own life and in relation to the difficult experience. The second example also invites the youth to make richer meaning of sadness, transforming it from a negative effect to an expression of what matters.

Let's take a closer look. Consider the chart below. What are the differences in these questions? What kinds of answers might they elicit? Where do you imagine each conversation might go?

| *Effects-Based* | *Response-Based* |
| --- | --- |
| What happened next? | What did you do next? |
| Why did you shut down? | What skills did you use to control your feelings? |
| What makes you so angry? | What is anger a protest against? |
| How long were you checked out? | How did you know it was safe enough to come back? |
| Who else got picked on? | What did you do to take care of your friends? |
| How is this affecting you now? | How are you taking care of yourself now? |

Asking questions about responses is also part of attending to the absent but implicit as discussed in Chapter 5. Double listening (also presented in Chapter 5) prepares us to ask questions about young people's responses. When we doubly listen, we pivot from the single story of effects and engage in a rich story of a young person's agency, one which opens conversational doors to their hopes, intentions, and values (that's where on point curiosity comes in, too). Response-based questions are a powerful resource to story young people's acts of resistance and bring forward their author-ity from behind the curtain of oppression.

## Summary

Curiosity puts into action constructionist theory and ethics. Through the intentional use of questions, curiosity functions as the engine of praxis, driving conversations toward new possibilities and positioning youth and youth worker alike to engage in a kind of wonder that takes them from "the known and familiar" toward "what is possible...to know" (M. White, 2007, p. 271). Without curiosity, we not only compromise our opportunity to discover amazing things with and about young people, but we also fail to live into our ethic of centering young people's knowledges and encouraging their own agency.

Questions carry curiosity into conversations. The questions that you ask emerge from your relationship with youth, reflecting the language, aesthetic, and interests of the young people you're engaged with. Cultivating a narrative practice of curiosity that features skillful questioning requires ongoing practice.

## Highlights

### From a statement-driven practice to a question-driven practice

| Questions | Statements |
| --- | --- |
| **Bring forward** | |
| Possibilities | Certainties |
| Multiple stories | Single story |
| **Positioning** | |
| Not-knowing | Knowing better than |
| Co-researcher | Expert |
| Decentered/influential | Centered/influential |
| Curiosity, wonder | Certitude |
| **Attention to power and discourse** | |
| Question assumptions | Maintain assumptions |
| Share discursive power | Hold discursive power |

## Key Terms

1. **Curiosity:** A desire to wonder beyond what we know by suspending assumptions, questioning taken-for-granted understandings, and staying open to multiple perspectives and meanings.
2. **Not-knowing approach:** This stance allows us to stay curious by avoiding quick conclusions or being "too quick to know." It does not mean that

you don't know anything; it means you suspend your assumptions and strive to learn more through active curiosity.

3. **Response-based approach:** A response-based approach is based on the idea that people always respond and exercise agency, even in the face of oppression, violence, or other traumatic events. By asking *response-based questions*, we bring forward the responses youth make as meaningful acts of resistance and expressions of what matters to them. This is in contrast to conventional practices that feature *effects-based questions*. These questions focus on the effects on youth of oppressive events.

## Discussion Questions

1. What's one of the best questions someone ever asked you, one that made you say, *that's a good question*, and got you thinking about something completely new? What was that experience like? What did it make possible?

2. Take a look at the different kinds of questions presented in this chapter. Which ones seem most familiar, and which ones are most novel? Why do you suppose that is? What kinds of questions are you most interested to integrate into your youth work practice? What about these questions appeals to you? What questions do you have a hard time picturing in your practice? What do you make of that?

3. In Chapter 5, I introduced Michael White's (2000) ideas of absent but implicit and double listening. You may recall that the concept of absent but implicit is based on the idea that any expression (the present and explicit) is in relation to something else—the absent but implicit. Revisit the list of expressions on page 102 and practice asking questions that reflect doubly listening to the expression.

4. Throughout the book, there are vignettes and examples that use a variety of questions. Have a "question scavenger hunt" where you take the list of types of questions presented in this chapter to search throughout the book for some examples of each kind.

## Notes

1 Chapter 10 covers deliberate practice in depth.

2 Paré (2013) suggests we understand questions as existing on a continuum from "fairly open to very closed" (p. 120). Simply by posing a question, the person asking has had a hand in determining some extent of the response: every question points people toward a field of responses.

3 I use *figure* here, not *person*, deliberately. Youth can be in meaningful relationships with others who may or may not be actual living persons in their lives. I have inquired about the perspectives of sports heroes and superheroes, comic book characters and stuffed animals, family pets and childhood imaginary friends, among others. What matters is the regard with which the young person you're engaged with holds the relationship and that the other party may have a perspective that is valuable to bring forward.

# 8

## YOU GOT A PROBLEM? LANGUAGE FOR PROBLEMS AND PROTESTS

> All the facts only belong to the problem, not to its solution.
> *Ludwig Wittgenstein*, Tractatus Logico-Philosophicus

> Problems are stories and "bad behavior" is a performance of those stories.
> *Angela, a youth worker*

Sometimes in youth work, as in life, things don't always go well. Whether a group of young people isn't clicking and frustrations flare; or someone (youth and/or youth worker) is having a bad day; or the effects of systemic oppression are taking their toll on young people, youth workers, their relationships, and their activities together, there will be times when you'll need to respond to painful and difficult situations. This is true regardless of the context you work in and the youth you serve.

In addition to the hard stuff that can show up in the best of circumstances, more and more youth workers are providing services for youth who experience issues that adversely affect their health, safety, and dignity. Although youth workers are not explicitly positioned to work as psychotherapists, many do provide services to young people who have psychiatric diagnoses or have otherwise been labeled as having "behavioral" or "mental health" problems.

Often, youth workers I encounter say they feel that they don't have the knowledge and skill set to support youth who experience depression and anxiety, relationship challenges, chemical misuse, the effects of trauma, and other problems. Responding to this desire to know more is not a matter of outfitting youth workers with information on diagnoses and the psychological treatment du jour; on the contrary, I want to see youth workers *do* youth work, not therapy. At the heart of youth work is taking a stand distinct from—sometimes in opposition to (Skott-Myhre, 2008)—the decontextualized and individualist conceptualizations of identity that are characteristic of Western psychotherapy (J. White, 2015). The relationships and opportunities that emerge within a youth work context offer young people a place where they are free to bring *all of themselves* and not fall subject to the normative gaze and notions of "personal improvement" and psychologization (Parker, 2007, p. 2) that are the central projects of the psychiatric-social service industry.

What keeps youth workers from seeing themselves as prepared to support young people with "mental health"[1] concerns? One thing that gets in their way is an unquestioning acceptance of the dominance of the medicalization of the problems people experience. By *medicalization,* I mean the ways that Western society has come to understand problems (and the struggles and suffering they cause) as matters of the body (and, in the case of "mental health" specifically, the "mind"). As such, they come under the scrutiny of medical research and treatment. This is not a youth worker problem. It's a problem born out of the medical industry's success at gaining hegemonic status and insinuating itself into our daily lives.[2] This success fits nicely with our cultural assumption of an internalized, essential self. Thus, because youth workers don't question the authority of the medical industry and the veracity of its claims, they're apt to view work with youth who are strapped with informal or formal diagnoses as the province of mental health professionals.

This unquestioned acceptance is one place where the gap between youth workers' analysis of power and the doing of youth work is often most apparent. It's a place where youth and youth workers alike obediently accept psychiatry's thinly described labels as telling The Whole Truth, without asking the questions they often pose when confronting systems of power such as racism, heteronormativity, and patriarchy. Not asking questions speaks to the omnipotence and omniscience of the discourse of medicalization. Why do we blindly accept the constructs of an industry that gave us *drapetomania*[3] and pathologized sexual desires and practices that deviated from a limited notion of "normal" (thus, constructing homosexuality as a psychiatric disorder) until 1973?[4] It's my contention that youth workers—when equipped with an analysis of power operations and narrative practices that align with this analysis—occupy a unique and critical position to offer meaningful and transformational engagements with youth who seek to reclaim their lives from a host of problems.

Indeed, the scrappy, relationally focused, youth-centered, intentionally political project that is youth work can provide refuge for young people experiencing the all too frequent impersonal and depoliticized "helping" of the social service-psychiatric-big pharma-correctional-industrial complex. Specifically, this means understanding problems in context and seeing youth as not defined by their problems, but rather, seeing them in resistance to their problems. This absolutely does not mean that we deny problems or their effects. It does mean that we question how we construct problems and where we locate them (J. White, 2015). From a constructionist stance, we understand problems as contextual and situated in the social world, not "inside" people. This is not merely a philosophical position; it is a political and ethical one as well.

As we focus on praxis—the integration of the knowing, doing, and being of youth work—constructionist philosophy and post-structural theory come to life through the practices they inform and the reflexivity they encourage. The ideas and practices presented thus far (e.g., storying, dialogue, double listening, absent but implicit, experience-near descriptions, confirming meaning, curiosity, intentional questions, and response-based practice) are embodiments of the many concepts presented in Part I.

One of the core concepts within social construction and post-structural theory is the *nonessential "self"* discussed in Chapter 1. This is often one of the most challenging concepts for people to grasp, as it explodes so much of what we take for granted within modernist ideology about who we *are*. You may "get it" in the abstract and see its liberatory potential, but wonder, *how do I DO that?* What does it look like (and sound like) to have a conversation that really reflects the idea of a discursively produced, nonessential identity? How do we talk about the *stuff* that makes people, well, *people*?

Chapter 8 introduces *externalizing* (M. White, 1986; M. White & Epston, 1990), a language practice that embodies and reflects the concept of the nonessential self to its fullest. In youth work, the use of externalizing opens new possibilities for young people to exercise agency, engage with accountability, and leverage their creativity. Externalizing conversations help youth expose systems of oppression and reclaim their identities from problem-saturated stories that disregard context and power relations. As such, externalizing is a conversational resource that engages with the politics and ethics of liberatory youth work.

## The Who, What, When, Where, and Why of Externalizing* (*not necessarily in that order)

> I tell them, you don't have to accept labels as your identity and the stories told about you aren't you.
>
> *Mickella, a youth worker*

As noted before, Michael White first introduced the idea of externalizing in his therapeutic work with children and families in Australia. He furthered this practice through his collaboration with David Epston, a Canadian expat in New Zealand. Since then, practitioners in psychotherapy (for example, Brown & Augusta-Scott, 2007; Flaskas, McCarthy, & Sheehan, 2007; Freedman & Combs, 1996; Madigan, 2011; Nylund, 2000; Zimmerman & Dickerson, 1996), community work (Monroe, Reynolds, & Playmondon, 2013; Sliep, 2003; Wingard, Johnson, & Drahm-Butler, 2015), conflict mediation (Monk & Winslade, 2012; Winslade & Monk, 2000), and youth work (Hartman, Little, & Unger, 2008; Little, Hartman & Ungar, 2007; McEwen, 2017) use externalizing conversations in their varied settings. While the many conversational practices that I've introduced thus far come from a range of constructionist-informed approaches organized around the narrative or story metaphor, externalizing is a practice particular to Michael White and David Epston's pioneering work. It is the hallmark of their narrative approach.

Specifically, externalizing conversations involve separating people from problems, both conceptually and linguistically. Michael White noted that conventional language practices informed by the modernist notion of an essential "self" collapse problems onto people's identities. People either *have* a problem or they *are* a problem (Madsen & Gillespie, 2014). White wanted to engage with people in a way that didn't require them to submit to the totalizing effects of locating problems in people. He developed the practice of externalizing so that people could experience themselves in ways other than those defined by the problems in their lives.

For example, a young person may say, "I have anxiety," or "I'm anxious." They may go on to talk about themself as "an anxious person" or say, perhaps, "it's just how *I am*." This reflects the structural notion that the "self" is inside of us and understands anxiety as a trait attached to that self. From a modernist perspective, the internalized self represents our "true nature" and it is where everything happens. We locate problems, personalities, characteristics (good and bad), skills, and our "mind" inside of us.

Locating problems inside of young people leads to a totalized identity (as discussed in Chapter 2), one which excludes other stories or ways people are in the world not accounted for by the problem story. As such, this way of talking and describing problems does not reflect constructionist philosophy or post-structural theory. More important—because the intention here is not theoretical purity for purity's sake—the language practices (and the ideas that inform them) that locate problems inside of people often engender shame and hopelessness, lead people to assume identities defined by problems, and push other identity conclusions to the margins.

Think for a moment about a time when someone approached you about something you had done that concerned them. Perhaps a family member feels mad that you missed several family events and calls you "irresponsible," or maybe your friend thinks you are quick to get into fights and says you're "an angry person." If you feel at all blamed, or have a sense that "this is just how I am or who I am," you may not see any hopeful way to address these concerns.

Externalizing is an alternative language practice that locates problems (and, as we will see, also so-called strengths and preferred characteristics) in the social world where people are in relationship with them. We no longer view problems as traits or representations of a person's essential and "true nature;" rather, we view problems as social constructs that emerge from a particular context and history (Carey & Russell, 2002). This makes greater agency possible, as youth—their identities now separated from the problem(s)—can take action against or in protest of the things that make trouble for them. This agency replaces the hopelessness that commonly occurs with internalized conclusions.

Take the previous example of a youth who says that they're "anxious." We can externalize this by saying, for example, "Anxiety[5] is giving you lots of trouble," or "Anxiousness makes this hard for you." When we externalize problems in this way, youth have space to consider how the problem affects their lives. They also can examine how they have influence over the problem and where they can exercise agency. We may ask, "what do you do to keep Anxiousness from completely taking over?" Externalizing in this way places the young person and Anxiousness in relationship with each other in the social world, opening pathways to alternative stories other than the totalizing account of an anxious person.

Let's pause and give externalizing a test drive in the activity below.

---

### Externalizing Activity

Chose something about yourself—a trait or a feeling—that you don't like, or think you have too much of, or others complain about. Think of it as a description in *adjective* form, such as, "competitive," "judgmental," "skeptical," "guilty," or "lazy." In the questions below, replace "X" with your trait or feeling.

1. How long have you been ⁞
2. What are you most X abou
3. Have you been X at other t            ur life?
4. How do you feel about beir
5. What other problems have ⟨            your being X?
6. What led to your being X?

Take the same trait/feeling you us            ut change it from an adjective to a *noun*. "Competitive" becom            ɛtitiveness," "judgmental" becomes "judgment," "skeptical" be            ɛpticism," etc.
   Replace "y" in the questions be.ᴜᴡ with your noun.

1. When would you say you first noticed Y in your life?
2. When is Y most likely to take over?
3. What is it that invited Y to make trouble in your life?
4. When Y is pushing you around, what might you do that you wouldn't typically do?
5. How has Y affected your job, relationship, and family?
6. What does Y want you to forget about yourself?

*(Adapted from Freedman & Combs, 1996)*

What did you notice? What kinds of answers did each set of questions invite? How would you describe your experience of being asked each set of questions? What did it feel like? Where did the questions take you? What does each set of questions make possible?

Instead of collapsing problems onto young people's identities, the practice of externalizing makes problems available for scrutiny and exposure, and the conditions that invite and maintain problems become visible (Carey & Russell, 2002). When we locate problems in the relational world of discourse, we resist the burden of individualism and privatization of social problems (discussed in Chapter 1).

Externalizing is not merely a technical feat of linguistic gymnastics. If you treat it as a technique or gimmick divorced from a thorough understanding of the concepts we've covered so far, externalizing won't work. In fact, externalizing is a political and ethical practice of resistance to classification, which often comes in the form of psychiatric diagnoses or other normative notions of identity (Madigan, 2011). Externalizing is an active refusal of universalized and essentialist ideas about identity. It gives youth room to exercise greater agency and accountability. Externalizing is post-structural theory in action, as it leads us to ask questions about the effects of prevailing discourses and the problems they influence in young people's lives.

It's important to say a bit more about how externalizing increases accountability. People just learning about externalizing sometimes raise concerns that separating youth from problems "let's them off the hook." Individualism, inspired by capitalist metaphors, teaches us to "own" our problems and take personal responsibility for them (Parker, 2007). When we locate problems in youth, it is easy for them to collapse onto young people's sense of who they are. This leads to comments such as, "it's just who I am," or "I can't help it, it's how I am." Those are not the sentiments that typically invite someone to accountability.

On the other hand, when youth and problems are seen as distinct actors in relationship together, young people can step into accountability, in part because they feel they have agency to act in protest of the problem(s). They can assume accountability, rather than hopelessness, in how they navigate their relationship with problems. Even when a youth has a problem that will have an enduring or permanent impact on their lives, such us a chronic illness, they can experience agency and step into accountability around how they negotiate the relationship with the problem. This negotiation is really about *how they will story* their relationship with problems in their life.

For example, I once worked with a 10-year-old diagnosed as being on the Autism Spectrum. He told me that, although he knew the problems this condition created in life would always try to get the best of him, "like Voldemort," he had ways to resist it and always "fight back, just like Harry Potter" (Tilsen, Russell, & Michael, 2005). Before we externalized the problems and their effects, he was struggling under the weight of hopelessness and a lack of confidence. Through externalization he saw that he could act against the problem, and this helped him assume accountability.

---

### Internalized vs. Externalized Problems

Here are some examples of ways to take a statement made using internalized language and change it to an externalizing question.

| | |
|---|---|
| Those two are whiny, they complain about everything. | *How does Whininess get them to complain so much?* |
| I get so frustrated with the others. | *When does Frustration seem to show up the most?* |
| I got so nervous I puke the performance. | *What does Nervousness say or do to get you to puke?* |
| This place is racist. | *How is Racism a part of this place?* |
| I hate how they tease er kids. | *Why is Teasing something you stand against?* |
| I feel embarrassed bec w they are judgy abou es and talk behind my t | *How does Talking Behind Your Back and Judginess get you to feel embarrassed?* |
| I can't concentrate bec ADHD. | *What are some of ADHD's ways of stealing your concentration?* |
| She says I'm a sexist! | *How do you think she sees Sexism showing up in your relationship?* |
| I can't go on the outing because I hit that kid. | *Has Hitting gotten you to do things you've regretted before?* |

---

## Externalizing: Not Just for Problems

> I ask youth, what stuff do you want to have as part of the stories that you like about yourself?
>
> *Angela, a youth worker*

We don't only externalize problems or things that give us trouble; we also externalize the good stuff, so-called strengths, or positive characteristics. The reason we do this is because we'd be theoretically dishonest if we didn't. We can't conceptualize a nonessential self, one which is discursively produced in the relational world, if we view our preferred qualities as being "natural" or "just who we are." Practically speaking, if we internalized the good stuff, we'd cheat ourselves (and the youth we work with) out of important conversational resources for meaning making and standing up to problems.

This is an important point. Often when people are first learning to have externalizing conversations, they focus on separating people from problems—and this is good, for the many reasons discussed before. However, it's just as important to make sure that we don't fall into the trap of locating the ways of being that young people prefer or consider to be "a positive" *inside of them*. If we do, we run some of the same risks associated with essentialist identities that we face when we locate problems in people. We miss out on the opportunity for rich descriptions of what matters about a particular quality or way of being, its history, who has contributed to it, and what they hope to do with it (Carey & Russell, 2002).

---

## Internalized vs. Externalized Preferred Qualities

Here are some examples of ways to take a statement made using internalized language about a preferred quality and change it to an externalizing question.

| | |
|---|---|
| Being confident helped me try something new. | *What role did Confidence play in your willingness to try something new?* |
| We feel really strongly about their homophobic policies. We're Passionate about it. | *How will Passion help challenge these policies?* |
| I just know how to survive so I do what I have to. | *Where have you learned yours Skills of Survival?* |
| That's just who I am—I don't take shit from anyone. | *How does being a Refuser-of-Shit help you deal with the crap at school right now?* |

---

## Externalizing Conversations in Action: The Political is the Personal

> It's important to help them understand that powers that are invisible are everywhere, and you can only interrogate and interrupt something when it's made visible.
>
> *Eli, a youth worker*

When we externalize problems, we actively situate youth and their lived experiences in the social world. That is, we see young people as being in *relationship with* the things that make trouble for them. We also place this relationship in the social world that influences the youth, the problem, and their relationship. This is a practice of contextualizing. When we internalize problems, we disappear the discursive political contexts that produce them. This contributes to the gap between an analysis of power operations and practice that I've mentioned previously.

---

### #FergusonSyllabus Question

Marginalized youth have many problem-saturated stories collapsed onto their identities, leading to totalizing descriptions. How can externalizing be viewed as an act of resistance to systems of oppression?

---

What does it look like to align our analysis with our practice? How can externalizing help us realize this? Let's consider two examples.

## Standing up to a Reign of Fear: Interviewing Homophobia

The administrator of a high school asked me to work with some of the student body leaders who wanted to respond to an increase in homophobic comments and threats. The students named Homophobia as the problem, so we externalized Homophobia. One of the activities we planned was an interview of Homophobia.[6] We talked about the kinds of things they might want to know about Homophobia, and I suggested some questions they could use as starter questions. I asked them to think about what Homophobia would look like, how it would dress, what it would sound like, what things it would be interested in, etc. so that they would have a "profile" of Homophobia.

Then, two students stood in as embodiments of Homophobia (they called themselves *Homo* and *Phobia* respectively). *Homo* assumed an aggressive and confrontational attitude while *Phobia* presented himself as worried and disgusted. They took questions from the other students.

The students asked questions to understand Homophobia's history, its ways of working, the conditions that maintain its presence, its tactics, and ways the students themselves may contribute to Homophobia's Reign of Fear (as one of the students called it) in their school. Below are some example questions (feel free to imagine ways in which Homophobia might answer these!):

- How long have you been around in general, and when did you come to our school?
- What made you feel like you could show up here?
- What is your goal for being at our school?
- Are there certain things about our school, the adults here, or how it runs that makes you think you can spread Homophobia here?
- Who sponsors your work here? How do they benefit from the hurt you cause?

- Who are your partners that help you hurt our queer classmates and teachers? Are there certain ideas or attitudes or actions that you like to hang around with?
- What do you do to convince some kids and adults to carry out your plans?
- How do you get other kids who don't want to be part of your Homophobia group to do your dirty work?
- When are you most likely to try to get away with putting down the queer people in our school? Why is this your favorite time and place?

These questions changed the conversation about homophobia dramatically. Prior to the externalizing conversation, students would call other students *homophobes* or describe them as *homophobic*. Locating the problem in other students created an "us vs. them" dynamic that ignored complexity and context. It also assumed that the only people affected by homophobia are those *attacked* by it. When we locate problems in the social world, we're all affected by them, but in different ways and to varying degrees.[7]

For example, in the interview with *Homo* and *Phobia,* the students discovered that Homophobia relies on the complicity of students who don't take an active stand against Homophobia (even if they also do not engage directly with it), and on the microaggressions embedded within heteronormative assumptions made by both youth and adults (e.g., assuming opposite gender romances or that students' parents were straight). These discoveries helped the youth realize that *even some of them*—the students seeking ways to stop Homophobia—were at times unwitting contributors to Homophobia's presence in their school.

As the interview continued, the group interspersed questions about how to stand up to Homophobia along with more inquiries about Homophobia's operations. These questions shed light on small but significant things that students were already doing to challenge Homophobia. The interview also shed light on new ways to stand against it. This brought forward alternative stories to the single story of Homophobia's dominance. Here are some questions that students asked Homo and Phobia:

- What are some things you've heard around school that make you think your reign of fear could come to an end?
- When and where have you felt most unwelcomed at school? What about that experience had you feeling like you couldn't stick around?
- What kinds of ideas, attitudes, or actions do some students and adults use that keep you from making even more trouble?
- What's been an embarrassment for you, a time when your plans to humiliate others failed?
- If the school offered a course on resisting Homophobia, what would some of the lesson plans be?
- What's the thing you don't want to hear come from the administration because it would signal the downfall of your plans? What don't you want to hear from faculty? Students? Parents?

The students used the information from the interview to help them create ways to address the problem of Homophobia and invite students into accountability without locating the problem inside people. They were able to leverage their understanding of what sustained Homophobia and what countered it in efforts to cultivate an inclusive and welcoming school climate.

### Not Buying It: Anxiety and Capitalism Meet the Spirit of Ultimate

The second example of how an externalizing conversation contextualizes problems and invites exploration of power involves a consultation with Brendon, a 20-year-old white cisgender male. Brendon was in his first year as a full-time coach of a youth ultimate frisbee team through a youth sports program. He was passionate about ultimate and committed to being a great coach and role model. As the competition season approached, Brendon found himself captured by worries. He was experiencing many physical manifestations of what he called "Anxiety" and his confidence as a coach was slipping. Brendon and his supervisor, Tanesha, had the idea to invite me to meet together with them to find ways to support Brendon to resist Anxiety's grip on him.

We met for a consultation and discussed Anxiety and the trouble it was making. We had an externalizing conversation where we carefully tracked the ways Anxiety was showing up in his life, and especially in his coaching. Brendon identified specifics such as worries and doubts about his abilities as a coach and youth worker; second-guessing himself; and upset stomach, sweating, trouble breathing, and pounding heart while interacting with the youth.

Tanesha also noticed that Anxiety got Brendon to "be quiet about sharing what he knows with other youth workers. He's usually a leader that way." This led to an exploration about what Anxiety tries to get Brendon to forget he already knows. Brendon said, "Anxiety has stories about me that don't include the things that I know about being a good coach." Together, Brendon and Tanesha identified some of the things that Anxiety leaves out about Brendon as a coach. I asked Brendon to keep on the lookout for stories that Anxiety spreads about him that omit these important things. I encouraged him to consider how Tanesha, his colleagues, and the youth he works with see him, and how their stories about him differ from those Anxiety tells.

I followed up with Brendon a few weeks later during my visit to the youth center. He said that things had been going much better since we talked and that Tanesha had been very helpful "calling out Anxiety when it tried to kick my ass." I was interested in knowing what he had been doing to stand up to Anxiety. Here is a portion of our conversation, one that highlights the connection between the problem of Anxiety and its relationship to broader cultural issues.

BRENDON: The more battles I win from Anxiety the better, but it's still there every day and it's exhausting.

JULIE: What have you been doing to win some from Anxiety and keep after it every day?

BRENDON: I'm constantly denying the stories Anxiety tells me.

JULIE: How are you denying the stories Anxiety tells you?

BRENDON: I try to remember that Anxiety sells stories that aren't true.

JULIE: Anxiety sells stories, like products or commodities?

BRENDON: Yes!

JULIE: What kind of relationship do you see Anxiety having with Capitalism?

BRENDON: Anxiety's relationship with capitalism is the constant pressure capitalism puts on people to produce; it's dehumanizing, it's impossible to meet the expectation of infinite growth, so when you don't meet it: enter Anxiety.

JULIE: That's quite the Marxist analysis! Have you thought of this before, this relationship between Anxiety and Capitalism?

BRENDON: Not really. Not until you asked. But I did have a psychology teacher once say that Anxiety is a problem of "what if?" and not "what is" and so I think that "what if" is the only thing that is truly infinite, and Anxiety gets me worried about "what if."

JULIE: What are the effects of these worries about the "what if" that Anxiety imposes?

BRENDON: It makes self-esteem not possible. Capitalism makes you feel you can produce anything but that you're not deserving of what you produce.

JULIE: Is this one of those false stories that Anxiety sells, that you're not deserving? Is Anxiety operating as a distributor for Capitalism?

BRENDON: Yes. And this week, I thought I wouldn't deserve to hold a good practice because I hadn't prepared enough, I didn't really have a plan. But we had a great practice. Some of the players told me how much they liked it.

JULIE: Is having a great practice another example of some of the wins you've had this week?

BRENDON: Yes.

JULIE: What would your players say they most appreciated? What made it a good practice for them?

BRENDON: I kept it open and flexible, like responding to how it was going, what they seemed to need at the time. In the past, Anxiety had me think I had to follow a strict plan that I prepared beforehand.

JULIE: In the absence of a lot of preparation and a plan, what helped you run a good practice? Was there anything that you reclaimed or that emerged as a resource for you when you resisted Anxiety's insistence on having a plan?

BRENDON: A kind of confidence. I was reclaiming confidence and relying on my knowledge and skills instead of a plan.

JULIE: So, maybe the untrue story Anxiety was selling was that you needed a plan because you didn't have skills and knowledge?

BRENDON: Yes, and when I bought that plan I paid for it with my confidence.

JULIE: How long have you been involved with ultimate as a player and coach?

BRENDON: Seven years.

JULIE: Are there other sports that you've been around, as a player, coach, or fan? Other sports you have experience with and knowledge of?

BRENDON: Yes—soccer for a few years before I got into ultimate.

JULIE: Do you think being a player prepares you in any way to coach?

BRENDON: Yes. I've had good coaches and bad coaches. And I think teachers have taught me about the kind of coach I do and don't want to be, too. There's a teaching element to coaching.

JULIE: OK, so over seven years' experience with sports and then like, what? 17 years' experience as a student... Is this a kind of preparation for coaching and running a practice?

BRENDON: Oh, yeah, that's totally true. I've spent lots of time with stuff that helps me coach.

JULIE: How is the kind of preparation that Anxiety sells, the kind that costs you confidence, different from the kind of preparation we're talking about here, this kind from your years as a student, an athlete, and an assistant coach?

BRENDON: Anxiety sells preparation for a cure-all, like it tells you that you have to be prepared for everything. You can't be prepared for everything. But that's why you have skills and knowledge. And I don't have to know everything all the time. I can seek others for advice. I can tell my players, "I don't know but I'll find out." I don't have to buy Anxiety's stories. They don't work and they should be off the market!

JULIE: As someone with a long and dedicated involvement with ultimate, how does your resistance to capitalism's intrusion into your relationship with ultimate fit with the ethos of the sport?

BRENDON: Totally! I was just thinking about that. I mean, ultimate is everything that capitalism isn't: it's about the spirit of the game, not hate-your-opponent competition and winning at all costs. That's why I love it. Damn. That's another thing Anxiety tried to get me to forget!

JULIE: Damn is right!

BRENDON: Yeah, I think I'll be good now as long as I remember what ultimate is about, and that it gives me confidence. I don't have to buy into Anxiety.

Going into this conversation with Brendon, I had no idea that Brendon would link his experience of Anxiety with capitalism, nor did I know that Brendon would offer such a rich understanding of how his experience with the problem of Anxiety relates to his understanding of the cultural meta-narrative of capitalism. As we saw from the conversation. Brendon hadn't thought of this himself *until I asked*.

How did I know to ask? Because I was focusing on having an experience-near conversation, I listened for his words and metaphors. Thus, when Brendon said that "Anxiety sells stories," I confirmed his meaning of the word "sells." His confirmation provided an entry point to explore his ideas about the ways capitalism influences Anxiety. In doing so, we created further space between

Brendon and the problem by solidly locating it within the discourse of capitalism. Brendon was able to take a stand against Anxiety—a problem located in the discursive world, not something that is part of him—using the resources of his skills and knowledge of ultimate, the confidence these bring him, and the relational ethic inspired by the sport he loves.

## Pro Tips and Cautions: Making Your Relationship with Externalizing Work

> You've got to believe that identities are flexible and fluid and can be constructed before youth can believe it.
>
> *Emily, a youth worker*

As a language practice, externalizing feels weird at first. Personifying or anthropomorphizing ideas typically understood as characteristics or qualities core to who people *are* directly challenges our conventional conversational practices. In fact, Winslade and Monk (1999) suggest that externalizing conversations are parodies of our dominant culture's "deficit thinking that pathologizes people and requires that they embrace a sense of hopelessness, shame, or guilt" (p. 36).

How can we get through the weirdness and embrace the parodic challenge to these prevailing discourses of deficit and individualism? To begin with, give yourself credit for getting this far in this book—digesting the tenets of post-structural theory and social construction provides the necessary footing for stepping into externalizing conversations. To help you step further into externalizing conversations (with Weirdness as an ally, not a barrier), here are a few pro tips for you to try:

1. *Get good with the theory.* In order for externalizing to work for you and youth, it cannot be just a technique to you. You have to embrace—in your head, heart, and gut—the notion of the nonessential self. This includes always looking to understand how personal narratives are situated in and influenced by discourses. It also means that you can't call your roommate "lazy" or your supervisor a "micromanager." Conceptualizing the nonessential self is a way of showing up in the world in all relationships.
2. *Practice.* Be kind to yourself, this is new. Let yourself engage with Learning. Practice with the activities in this chapter. How might you use externalizing to address concerns between you and your roommate or your supervisor?
3. *Acknowledge the weirdness.* When talking with youth, be transparent and let them know why you're externalizing. For example, you might say, "Hey I know this totally sounds weird, but what if we talked about 'Going Off' like it's a thing that pushes you around, not like it's part of you? This might help us—can we try?"

4. *Use a variety of means to personify and anthropomorphize.* In addition to naming problems and having externalizing conversations that track youth's relationships with them, ask youth questions that help them further personify the problem. For example, ask about what the problem looks like: does it have eyes and legs? How big is it and what does it sound like? Invite young people to draw the problem, and then to put themselves in the picture in relationship to the problem. You can do the same with the qualities, skills, and knowledges that you externalize together. Invite Creativity into the conversation and let it do its thing.

5. *Practice connecting specific problems to the discourses that produce and sustain them.* This helps us shift from looking through a microscope at individuals to looking through a telescope to see context. Enlist the young person to find out more about their context so that, together, you can see what discourses are influencing the particular problem they're facing.

6. *Take care with expressions of feelings.* Be cautious about externalizing anger, guilt, shame/embarrassment, or hurt *as problems.* Externalizing these feelings as expressions of what matters to the young person, or as responses to difficult events, is a good approach (recall absent but implicit, double listening, and response-based practices). This allows youth to describe the situation that brought on the feelings, and that situation can be externalized as a problem (Winslade & Monk, 1999).

7. *Partner with other practices.* As we saw in the example before, externalizing conversations don't exclude the use of other practices. You won't be able to externalize effectively if you leave Curiosity at home or if Impatience is coming between you and Compassion.

8. *Practice.* Nurture a meaningful relationship with a reflexive and deliberate practice (covered in Chapter 10).

## Summary

Externalizing conversations are unique to narrative approaches. Externalizing puts into relational action the conceptual notion of a nonessential self, and in so doing, opens conversational pathways to new and hopeful identity conclusions. By partnering with young people to put discursive space between themselves and the problems in their lives, youth workers provide enhanced opportunities for youth to assume accountability and author-ity in their lives. Furthermore, externalizing preferred qualities, skills, and knowledges allows youth to generate rich descriptions of the resources that help them protest problems and stand for what matters in their lives.

When we effectively externalize both problems and preferences, we actively situate the lived experiences of youth within the larger social world, and in particular, within the discourses that influence their lives. As such, externalizing is a promising liberatory practice that resists the privatization of social problems and invites youth and youth workers to stand together against totalizing stories of deficit, pathology, and disease.

## Highlights

### From Internalizing to Externalizing Conversations

| Internalized | Externalized |
| --- | --- |
| Authentic self | Preferred identities |
| Problems become identity | Problems are problems |
| "Good" qualities and "Strengths" are natural and fixed | Preferred identities are flexible and contextual |
| Adjectives that describe person | Nouns that person is in relationship with |
| "Owning behaviors" | "Engaging in practices" |

## Key Terms

1. **Externalizing:** Externalizing is the conversational practice that reflects the concept of the nonessential self. Instead of seeing problems and qualities as being inherent to people, or as "natural," we locate them in relationship with people in the social world. This prevents problems from collapsing onto identities and it makes preferred qualities and skills available as flexible resources to draw on. Externalizing helps us contextualize problems and preferences and consider power operations. Externalizing can help challenge totalizing stories and create possible new stories.

2. **Internalizing:** Internalizing is the conversational practice that reflects the concept of the essential self with an "authentic" interior. Qualities and problems are located "inside" people and collapsed onto their identities. This tends to ignore or minimize contextual influences and power operations, thus imposing the burden of individualism.

## Discussion Questions

1. How would you describe your current relationship with Externalizing?
2. If you and Externalizing were to sit down and have coffee, what do you think you'd talk about? What would you want to know about Externalizing? What would you want Externalizing to know about you?
3. What do you think Curiosity, Double Listening, and some of the other practices discussed would hope to happen if you introduced them to Externalizing?
4. What stories have there been about you that you would like to invite Externalizing into a conversation about?

## Notes

1 I put "mental health" in quotes because, from a constructionist and post-structural perspective, it is a highly problematic term and concept. It assumes that problems occur inside of people, that there is such a thing as a "mental" or "psychological" state or condition that exists outside of the social–relational world, that there is a distinction (rather than a mutually influential relationship) between what we construct as "mental" and "physical" health, and that efforts to address these problems focus inward rather than in the social–relational world.

2 It is beyond the scope and purpose of this book to offer full critiques of the medicalization of people's lives and identities, psychiatric diagnoses, and treatments. For more on this, see: Frances (2013), Greenberg (2013), Krish (2010), Watters (2010) and, Whitaker and Cosgrove (2015).

3 Drapetomania was the diagnosis created by Dr. Samuel Cartwright in 1851 to describe the "mental illness" that caused people in slavery to run away from enslavement.

4 The American Psychiatric Association removed homosexuality as a psychiatric diagnosis (i.e. psychopathology) in 1973.

5 Always use the word or term that the young person selects to externalize. This might be a collaborative process that includes asking the simple and important question, "what do you call the problem?"

6 It's common when externalizing problems to capitalize them as a way to emphasize their status as active agents separate from people.

7 I am not claiming that Homophobia affects a young person who uses homophobic slurs and bullying in the same or equal way as it does the queer youth threatened by the slurs and bullying.

# 9

# TURN IT UP

## Making Meaning of Pop Culture

It meant something to see people who looked like me in comic books.

*Ta-Nehisi Coates*[1]

If you're not seeing yourself reflected in pop culture, can you be beautiful?

*Andrea, a youth worker*

I don't think there's anyone who understands better than youth workers how important pop culture is to young people. Youth workers know that pop culture is youth culture, and that showing interest in youth's interests is central to relationship-making. What could become possible if youth workers took their engagement with youth and pop culture beyond relationship-making and into a richer and more complex conversational terrain, one that centers youth's meaning making and critical analysis of the culture industries?

This chapter presents practices from the interdisciplinary field of cultural studies. This innovate field offers conversational resources for meaningful engagement with youth about their relationships with pop culture. Sharing the same conceptual influences of constructionist philosophy and post-structural theory with the practices introduced thus far, cultural studies methodologies make a good fit with a narrative approach to youth work.

## Cultural Studies in the House

They'd want to just hang out and listen to hip-hop and get away from their white teacher and create an insular black space with their music.

*Sam, a youth worker*

Cultural studies is an interdisciplinary field that investigates the ways culture constructs and shapes everyday social interactions. By focusing on subjectivity and power, cultural studies seeks to understand culture (in all its forms) as situated within the social and political contexts that produce it. The field's influences include cultural anthropology, sociology, gender and queer studies, feminist theories, history, literary studies, communication studies, and economics (Barker, 2012). Cultural studies offers resources for deconstructing and making meaning of the multitudes of messages pumped out by the culture and media industries. In particular, cultural studies methodologies help youth workers and youth examine how the consumption of pop culture relates to ethnicity, class, race, sexuality, and/or gender (Tilsen & Nylund, 2016).

## Pop Culture: All the Things

> If what they're into isn't worth investigating, you're saying they don't matter… we're all breathing this stuff all the time.
>
> *Emily, a youth worker*

What am I referring to when I speak of *pop culture?* Pop culture (also referred to as *media culture*) is all the things. This includes all the things produced by the culture industries: TV, film, technology and social media, fashion trends, comics, video games, music, professional and NCAA sports, cosplay, and books. Often, one facet of the culture industry shares content with another, such as clothing with professional or NCAA team insignia, or merchandise produced in conjunction with a film or TV show (e.g., toys, clothing, or fast food meals). Finally, pop culture also includes social practices such as language vernaculars (e.g., *all the things, on point,* or *that's hot*), and memes.

All of the commodities and practices within pop culture produce texts, wherein a *text* is anything that produces meaning. Thus, a text needn't be comprised of words. For example, a text could be an image (such as the apple for Apple products, the Nike "swoosh," or the McDonald's arches) or a fashion style (such as hip-hop or grunge). The point is that we *make meaning* of these commodities because we have a relationship with them—whether or not we consume them directly or intentionally—and that we make meaning suggests the textuality of the product or social practice.

Finally, pop culture *is popular.* People share commodities, social practices, and texts that emerge from the culture industries through social interaction (both "in real life" and through social media). Among young people, this is especially true. Pop culture is nearly synonymous with youth culture, as youth literally explore, discover, define, and refine their identities and relationships using the Grand Central Station of pop culture: social media.

These definitions are useful in as much as they help determine what we're referring to when we talk about pop culture. Yet, from a cultural studies perspective, there are more meaningful and critical questions to consider, including:

- What does pop culture *do*?
- What are the effects of its doing?
- How do young people negotiate their relationship with pop culture and the meanings they make of their consumption?

By entertaining these questions, we can engage with youth in conversations about their relationships with pop culture and the meanings they construct about these relationships. Thus, we are less concerned with defining pop culture than we are with understanding the purposes it has in young people's lives (Barker, 2012). This is an important point of affinity between cultural studies and narrative approaches. The answer to the question, *"what does pop culture do?"* depends on who does the answering, and there are two competing schools of thought in regard to this. Let's take a closer look.

---

### Re-membering Me and My Stuff

- Thinking back to when you were a youth, what movies, TV shows, music, fashion, etc. did you consume?
- What meaning(s) did you make of your relationship with pop culture?
- What role did pop culture play in the shaping of your identity?
- Did you identify with a particular character? Song? How did that help you through a challenging time?
- What responses to your interests did the adults in your life have? How did their responses impact you?
- As an adult, how has your relationship with pop culture changed or stayed the same?

---

## The Popular Controversy

> The culture today is not mine, so I try to think about how I can show respect and listen to youth when I don't agree with them.
>
> *Marjaan, a youth worker*

The Frankfurt School (Adorno, 1991; Adorno & Horkheimer, 1979) represents one of the two opposing schools of thought. Social theorists from this intellectual tradition typically refer to *mass culture* and the *culture industries,* rather than "pop culture." This language places the emphasis on the influence of industry rather than consumers. The other perspective is that of cultural studies. Cultural studies favors the term *pop culture* because of the field's populist ethos and its focus on consumers' capacity for active meaning making. Thus, the controversy centers around the question of whether or not people are merely passive consumers of texts embedded within commodities by the producers, or are they an active, interpretive audience, both critiquing and producing meaning through consumption (Nylund, 2007; Tilsen & Nylund, 2009, 2016).

One can readily find studies or reports that convey concern about the negative effects of pop culture on young people. It's apparent that the people generating those reports would answer the question about what pop culture does by saying that it does harm.[2] This position represents the Marxist critique of the culture industries that comes out of the Frankfurt School. This perspective views consumers as dupes of the culture industries who lack the capacity to critique or resist the messages embedded within mass-produced commodities. The Frankfurt School maintains that the culture industries manipulate people into believing that they can achieve greater individuality through consumption of commodities and participation in the social practices associated with them. In fact, the Marxist analysis central to this perspective argues that standardization, not individuality, is advanced by the culture industries.

At the heart of the Frankfurt School's position is the emphasis on the production end of the culture industries. By focusing only on production and ignoring what consumers do through consumption, the assumption is that only texts embedded by producers influence the consumer. Thus, the Frankfurt School views people only as passive consumers, not as active producers of their own meanings. For example, this assumption is evident in claims that playing video games with violent content will reinforce *only* aggressive attitudes and behaviors, or that stories that feature a heroic man rescuing a damsel in distress will reinforce *only* patriarchal gender roles.

In contrast to the Frankfurt School, cultural studies theorists insist that meaning is made not only at production, but also through consumption, and that people are active agents in interpreting and constructing meaning (Fiske, 1989a, 1989b; Gauntlett, 2008; Hall, 1997; Willis, 1990). The meanings that youth make through consumption include *resistant meanings*. Resistant meanings are those that stand in opposition to dominant discourses and the influence of the culture industries (Gauntlett, 2008; Hall, 1997). Resistant meanings reflect the lived experiences and the unique circumstances of those who engage with any particular commodity. That meanings unique to individual's lives are made from a single text point to the *polysemic* quality of cultural texts (Hebdige, 1979). That is, texts hold many meanings. In other words, meaning is in the discursive world of the consumer. Consider these three examples:

1.  A black youth views the violence in video games not as a directive to shoot cops, but rather as validation of his anger toward an unjust system of police brutality and white supremacy. Playing these games allows him to "get my anger out toward the system in the game, not for real."
2.  A transgender youth finds community and validation of their identity in online communities and the blogs of other young trans people. This meaning stands against those often made by adults who view relationships cultivated through social media as inferior to those "in real life."
3.  A group of young women at a high school organize to wear tank tops to school in response to the school administration's ban on the garment for promoting "inappropriate exposure." The young women state that they reject the meaning imposed by the adults as one which objectifies and shames women's bodies. The meaning they make of the wearing of tank tops involves rejection of body shaming, and instead centers self-acceptance and pride. Furthermore, the young women point out that the school permits male-identified students to wear so-called "wifebeaters," a kind of sleeveless T-shirt. They assert that this administrative policy is rife with patriarchal and misogynist assumptions, not the least of which involves making women responsible for male's sexually violent activity.

Why is this important and what does it have to do with youth work? Within a consumer-based society, pop culture has achieved status as a dominant discourse. In fact, some social theorists and practitioners argue (Eko, 2003; Gauntlett, 2008; Monk, Winslade, & Sinclair, 2008) that it is the most influential cultural force shaping identity today. Youth share and circulate the products of the culture industries in a way that elevates the influence of *horizontal culture* (the practices shared among a peer group) over that of *vertical culture* (practices passed down through generations within a family system) (Maalouf, 2000). Pop culture is embedded with meanings that are typically saturated by normative specifications that reflect the prevailing meta-narratives of capitalism, white supremacy, patriarchy, heteronormativity and homonormativity, ableism, cissexism, nationalism, beauty and body specifications, and ageism. These texts reinforce certain norms, while they exclude, ridicule, pathologize, or vilify other identity possibilities that exist outside these norms.

Given its powerful influence, the question to ask is: *why wouldn't we talk about this?* It's not realistic to have conversations about class, race, gender, or for that matter, *anything* that has to do with identity without investigating the influence of pop culture. If we don't partner with youth in consideration of pop culture's importance to them and its influence on identity, we miss a critical piece of doing engaged, responsive, critical youth work.

## Cultural Studies Methodologies in Action: Getting Past "That's Cool"

> Young Thug wears a tutu. Twenty years ago, it was not possible for a black man—as an artist or consumer—to be openly queer and accepted in hip hop culture.
>
> *Marjaan, a youth worker*

As I said before, youth workers understand that pop culture matters to youth. Going beyond that understanding to enter the landscape of meaning making and critical analysis requires conceptual and conversational resources that get us past saying, "that's cool" and looking through a young person's Instagram posts with them. Cultural studies methodologies provide such resources. These methodologies offer critical media literacy skills for unpacking embedded meanings and generating alternative resistant meanings that help youth construct preferred identities.

The polysemic nature of cultural texts are central to a cultural studies approach. Stuart Hall (1973), a pioneer of cultural studies, contends that there are three positions from which people *decode*, or make meaning of, the *encoded*, or embedded, cultural texts. These positions are: *dominant, negotiated*, and *oppositional*.

*Dominant* readings are those in which the consumer agrees with the messages encoded at production. Examples of this position include, young people agreeing with or "buying into" the idea that female beauty is marked by thinness, whiteness, and subservience to men while reading fashion magazines, or believing that all black men are violent gangsters after listening to corporate rap music. The consumer aligns themself with the dominant point of view by accepting and decoding the meaning as it was encoded by the producers.

When youth make meaning from a *negotiated* position, they may accept some of the encoded messages within the text, but they also reject some as well. For example, youth may find the body and beauty specifications promoted in fashion magazines rife with harmful patriarchal and racist messages that they reject, while also enjoying the fashion styles and presentation of the photographic layout as artistic and skillful. Thus, they negotiate their relationship with the magazine's messages by both acknowledging the dominant messages (women must conform to beauty standards) and adapting their consumption to meet a preference of theirs (focus on art and technique). In regard to corporate rap, youth may reject the vilification of black men and romanticizing of criminality while also understanding that black rappers are performing a racist version of black identity that allows them to earn a living in a racist culture.

Readings from the *oppositional* position reject the encoded messages and make resistant meanings that oppose the intended message. Often, young people from marginalized backgrounds are likely to take up this position and render interpretations that reflect their social locations and lived experiences (Hall, 1981). Kellner (1995) suggests that young people often read "against the grain" of media by making their own meaning and using it for their own purposes.

For example, a young woman who rejects the beauty specifications of the fashion industry might read the images in a fashion magazine as pleas for help and a warning to others by women imprisoned by patriarchy. In this oppositional reading, the photos are not evidence of these woman promoting beauty standards; rather, they're evidence that they want others to know of the harmfulness of these standards. Or, black youth who reject the portrayal of black men by corporate rap as violent misogynists may take the oppositional position that corporate rap isn't teaching black men to be violent; rather, it is showing that black people know what white people think about them, and they're parodying white people's stereotypes and fears.

## Oppositional or Just Queer?

Borrowing from queer theory, I find it helpful to think about negotiated and oppositional readings as a *queering* of texts, particularly where gender, sexuality, or binary ideas about identity are at play. Queering a text means that we read it from a vantage point or in a way that unhinges assumptions about gender, sexuality, class, race, ability, body specifications, etc., and instead insert meanings that challenge or oppose those meanings. Queering is an act of resistance to normative identity specifications that typically saturate media texts.

Doty (1993) suggests the following questions as a way to analyze media texts through a queer cultural studies lens:

1. How does the product reinforce or disrupt traditional dichotomies and/ or associations among them (white/black, straight/gay, masculine/ feminine, male/female, good/evil)?
2. How does the product reinforce or disrupt the modern notion of "essentialist" (the idea that sexuality and gender is ahistorical and fixed in biology) gender or sexual identities?
3. How does the product reinforce or disrupt heterosexuality or its presumptions about the continuities, congruencies, or stability of the relationships between sex, gender, and desire?
4. Can this text be read against the grain to unearth hidden queer meanings and pleasures?

## Three-Pronged Approach

> If you believe you have to be culturally competent, this is a part of it.
>
> *Emily, a youth worker*

Cultural studies uses a triangulated or three-pronged approach to inquiry (Ang, 1996). The areas of inquiry and the kinds of questions asked resonate well with constructionist philosophy and narrative approaches. The three areas of inquiry include political economy, textual analysis, and audience reception.

*Political economy* involves analysis of production and distribution. Inquiry into the political economy of pop culture helps young people connect the things they buy with the industries that make, market, and profit from them. Investigation of political economy includes questions such as:

- Who do you think is responsible for creating these images of happy heterosexual couples?
- Do you think the producers of this music are interested in the way it portrays young black men?
- If you were a consultant to the fashion industry, what recommendations would you make so that people wouldn't feel "fat-shamed?"
- Who do you imagine is responsible for creating these images of black men as "thugs?"
- What kinds of companies own the TV shows that depict people within the male/female, hetero/homo binaries?
- Other than getting you to spend money on their clothes, do the CEOs of H&M, Aeropostale, Abercrombie, etc. have any interest in your life?
- If you were in charge of the music on a popular label, what kinds of songs would you produce?

This kind of questioning invites youth to consider that the texts and images they consume reflect certain values that come from the particular social and political location of the people behind the production of pop culture commodities.

---

### Black Enough for Gangsta Rap

During Marjaan's first week of work at a drop-in center for youth experiencing homelessness, Isaiah, a black youth, told him that he didn't think Marjaan was really black because he didn't "sound like he was from the 'hood." In fact, Isaiah told Marjaan, a proud black man, that he "sounded white." As Marjaan explored further, he discovered what Isaiah meant was that Marjaan sounded educated which, to Isaiah, conflicted with being black.

Marjaan asked him what black people "sound like," and Isaiah named another black male staff. "Then I asked him why he thought white people

*(Continued)*

get to own education, or sounding or being smart, and where his ideas about that were coming from," Marjaan said. "I also asked him if it's possible that there's more than one way to talk and still be black, and if there are more ways to be black besides how someone talks."

These questions led them to a discussion about the music Isaiah listened to and how it was shaping his ideas about black identity, and in particular, black male identity. Marjaan asked Isaiah, *who do you think makes that, who produces it, and whose ideas of black identity does corporate gangsta rap promote?* "We got to a place in the conversation where I said, *man, you watch too much TV! You're letting white people define Blackness*" Marjaan said.

Marjaan and Isaiah talked about the ways white people create the images of black men represented in rap music and TV. "I asked him, *are these your values, your family's values, your community's values? Who wins and who loses when white supremacy is behind these images? What are the effects on black people? On you?*"

The second domain of inquiry is *textual analysis*. This promotes discussion and critique of the values and messages encoded within specific popular texts. Through textual analysis, youth exercise agency by unpacking and critiquing the messages of the culture industry. This is central to cultural studies' emphasis on people having the capacity to be an active audience rather than passive consumers. Some examples of questions for textual analysis include:

- Who tends to be cast as the shooter and who is the victim in this game?
- What does the toy department's display suggest about who gets to play with what things?
- How are young people's relationships with teachers portrayed in this show?
- What relationships seemed to be approved of or celebrated in these ads?
- According to this film, what are the rules for being a man or women?
- What do these shows suggest about you and how you express gender?
- What message do you think the fashion industry wants you to get about bodies?
- What ideas about relationships do you get from these songs?

The third area of inquiry, *audience reception,* explores the ways young people make meaning of pop culture in their lives. Audience reception questions include:

- Despite the homonormative and cisnormative messages, what do you like about the show?
- What are some different versions of the lyrics that you've come up with? What do they say about what you think is important?
- What are some experiences in your life that may influence how you think about your choices of clothes?

- What are some things you've learned from the characters in this story?
- When you imagine yourself as part of the story, what difference do you make on what happens?

These questions can open space for individual meaning making. These meanings reflect young people's agency, preferences, and values. Audience reception questions bring forward negotiated and oppositional readings of cultural texts. This three-pronged approach provides youth workers with powerful conversational tools that invite young people into critical and political discussions about the things they consume and the meanings they make of these things. These tools also help youth workers take a decentered but influential position when engaging with youth around pop culture.

There is not a formula for asking questions in a particular order. What's asked, when it's asked, how it's asked, and if it's asked depends on the particular conversation. Thus, cultural studies is an apt resource for narrative youth work practice, as it remains flexible and responsive to the conversation at hand, while also paving the way for new and generative conversations.

---

### #FergusonSyllabus Question

What is important about engaging youth in critical conversations about their consumption of pop culture, and how can youth workers use the ideas and practices from cultural studies? How is this uniquely important for marginalized young people who may consume representations of themselves that promote problematic images and identities?

---

## Summary

Pop culture is youth culture, and the relationships youth have with the stuff of pop culture carry great significance in their lives. In as much as youth work is identity work, it is incumbent on youth workers to have meaningful and productive ways to talk with young people about these identity-influencing relationships. Cultural studies methodologies provide youth workers with the resources they need to partner with youth in these conversations. Because cultural studies shares the same constructionist and post-structural foundations that inform the other concepts and practices presented thus far, it is a fitting praxis ally for a narrative approach to youth work.

In particular, cultural studies-informed youth work is central in addressing issues of identity such as gender, race, class, sexuality, and ability in ways that center youth knowledge while helping them cultivate critical media literacy. These conversations highlight ways that young people are "critically active rather that passively uncritical" (Tilsen & Nylund, 2016, p. 230) in their consumption of media culture.

# Highlights

## *Seeking Multiple Meanings: Polysemic Texts and Youth Agency*

| Areas of Inquiry | | |
|---|---|---|
| Political Economy<br>*production side* | Textual Analysis<br>*deconstruction/critique* | Audience Reception<br>*meaning making* |

| Consumer Positions | | |
|---|---|---|
| Dominant<br>*Accept encoded meaning* | Negotiated<br>*Accept/reject aspects of*<br>*encoded meaning* | Oppositional/Queering<br>*Reject encoded/construct*<br>*resistant meaning* |

## Key Terms

1. **Cultural studies:** An interdisciplinary field that investigates the ways that culture influences everyday experiences and the ways citizens shape culture through their consumption of it.
2. **Dominant, negotiated, and oppositional readings:** These are the three positions from which consumers read media texts. *Dominant* readings are those in which consumers accept the meaning encoded at production; *negotiated* meanings are those in which consumers accept some encoded meanings but question or change others; and *oppositional* readings are those in which consumers contest or resist encoded meanings and instead make their own meanings of media text for their purposes.
3. **Polysemic:** From Greek, literally meaning "many signs." In reference to media texts, polysemy means that there are multiple meanings in the text.
4. **Pop/media culture:** Pop or media culture includes all of the commodities of the culture industries (such as TV, film, technology and social media, fashion trends, comics, video games, music, professional and NCAA sports, cosplay, and books) that are popular and shared widely among people.
5. **Three-pronged approach:** Cultural studies uses a three-pronged approach for deconstructing and making meaning of popular texts. The three areas of inquiry are: *political economy* (the production aspect of the culture industries), *textual analysis* (deconstruction and critique of messages embedded within media texts), and *audience reception* (the meanings people make of media texts).

## Discussion Questions

1. Recall your discussion about your engagement with pop culture as a young person ("re-membering me and my stuff on page 123"). What are

some questions you could ask your younger self about the political economy, textual analysis, and meanings made about those interests?

2.  As you consider the meanings you were making as a young person, identify the dominant, negotiated, and oppositional readings you engaged in.

3.  What questions could you ask important adults in your life about their relationship with you and the things you were interested in? What would you like to ask them about their own relationship with pop culture and influence it had on them?

4.  How do you imagine yourself using these ideas in your practice of youth work?

5.  What are you thinking you may like to "try on" first?

## Notes

1   Quoted in: Gustines, G. G. (2015, September 22). Ta-Nehisi Coates to Write Black Panther Comic for Marvel. *New York Times*.

2   *Effects studies* isolate and analyze a single media text (e.g., song lyric or movie plot) for what researchers assume to be harmful effects. They do not ask consumers what meanings they make of the text. The results of these studies are universal, one-size-fits-all interpretations that emphasize the harmfulness of the media studied (Gauntlett, 2008).

# PART III

# The Personal and Political Labor of a Youth Worker

Every moment is an organizing opportunity, every person a potential activist, every minute a chance to change the world.

*Dolores Huerta*[1]

What I do outside of my practice to make my practice better involves showing up for and witnessing other people who are interrogating the world.

*Eli, a youth worker*

Throughout this book, I've argued that good, ethical youth work requires youth workers to concentrate a critical lens back on themselves while also exchanging a metaphorical microscope for a telescope. In doing so, discourses and their influence on youth and youth work become visible. In short, this emphasis has been on the relationship between the personal and the political aspects of youth work—the tacking back and forth between a close-up view of what you're doing, and the influential discursive contexts from which what you do emerges. The final two chapters of this book expand on the personal—how you intentionally work to improve your practice—and the political—where youth work needs to operate in order to truly engage in transformative change.

Chapter 10 is about what you do to improve your practice, and provides answers to these questions:

- What activities push you to enhance your praxis so that you have more ways to be relationally responsible, form meaningful connections with young people, and maintain a critical practice?
- How do you become competent at the very specific practices presented in this book?
- How do you continually expand your knowledges and abilities?

Throughout the book there have been questions for discussion and activities that invite you to critically question what you know, or think you know. The questions previously introduced, along with the concept of inner dialogue (Chapter 5), provide conceptual resources for a reflexive stance that prepares you to interrogate… everything. Being able to maintain a reflexive stance while engaged with young people doesn't happen by accident. Effective use of the practices introduced in this book isn't the result of reading about them. Indeed, youth workers who have the dexterity to be reflexive about their reactions in the midst of deep engagement with young people, and who are skilled in the art and craft of a narrative approach, work hard to cultivate these skills. Chapter 10 offers ideas for developing a critical reflexive and deliberate practice that advances your knowledge, skills, and ways of showing up to youth work.

Chapter 11 brings this book to a close with encouragement to move your youth work practice beyond the bounds of the basketball court, wilderness trail, art room, shelter, and drop-in center, to the messy and contested spaces of community organizing and policy making. It is necessary to acknowledge that our conversations with young people will continue to fall short of full liberatory impact until we transform the constraints imposed by systems of regulation and oppression. This includes the institutional structures of youth-serving agencies themselves, as well as the policies and politics of the communities they exist in. This chapter presents ideas from youth workers involved in organizing and activism as *part of* the youth work they do. I argue that a primary goal of youth work is to partner with and support young people to shape and transform the social-political landscape into a better world, one rich in spacious conversations that generate a proliferation of possible identities for youth and youth workers alike.

# 10

## LEMME WORK ON THAT

### Cultivating a Reflexive and Deliberate Practice

I have created a life style that supports contemplation, service to words.

*bell hooks*[2]

We all have stuff. We have to take time to unpack it.

*Sunnie, a youth worker*

You're almost done with this book. You've covered a lot of ground, from theory, to practice, to the critical space we call praxis where the two converge. Now what?

Curiosity and critical thinking are central characteristics of a narrative approach. Supporting a critical and curious practice doesn't start and stop when you're in conversation with youth. Cultivating and maintaining a practice that extends critical curiosity to an examination of your assumptions and the contexts in which you work is essential to a praxis of accountability and a relational ethic attentive to power relations. This means that you engage with the world around you in and out of practice.

This chapter presents ideas to help you create and maintain a reflexive and deliberate practice. Reflexive practice requires we go beyond *thinking* about our work, to critically questioning ourselves and our work. Ensuring that we always take stock of what influences us, where we're coming from, what we are doing, and what our doing does (Foucault quoted in Dreyfus & Rabinow, 1982) is vital to an ethic of care. Deliberate practice also means that we commit to improving ourselves and our craft of youth work—even when we're away from our jobs.

## Reflexivity: Critical Questions for a Critical Practice

> I need to be as reflexive as possible. I need to understand myself and be a role model before I can expect that of them.
>
> *Sam, a youth worker*

The term *reflexivity* might be new to you, and I wouldn't be surprised if you're wondering if I mean *reflective*. I assure you that I do not mean reflective, and I do think it's important to talk about the distinction. The difference between reflexive and reflective is important, yet, the two terms are often conflated or taken to mean the same thing. They're not the same, and in the constructionist tradition and narrative approach to youth work, we are most interested in cultivating reflexivity.

In *reflection,* we think about something such as an event, thing, or person. When we think to ourselves, for example, "that's a beautiful tree," we are reflecting. Reflection is an individual act that occurs in the privacy of your "mind." It's what we call your inner dialogue. Reflection is a way of thinking about something that emphasizes what you notice without any questioning or critical thinking about it. The focus when we reflect is *outward.*

Let's consider an example from practice. You may reflect on an activity you did with a group of youth and the conversation it generated. Your thinking may be about what happened during the time together, how they seemed to get along and work things out, your frustration with the one kid who asked the same questions over and over, and your appreciation for the insightful comments of another participant. The questions typical of reflection include: *What happened? What did you notice? How did you feel? What did you think?* While these questions are about your experience, they do not require you to *question* your experience or consider other perspectives. Thus, reflection upholds individualism.

When we engage in *reflexivity,* instead of focusing outward, we turn our focus to ourselves to entertain critical questions about our experience. We hold a mirror to our practice and in particular, to the assumptions and influences that underpin what we think and what we do. Uncertainty and humility are characteristics of reflexivity, as it is a process of deconstructing our knowledge and our certainty.

For example, we may reflect on the "beautiful tree" we saw. We could ask ourselves critical questions such as: Would other people experience the tree the same as I do? How does my experience growing up around these trees lead me to find beauty in them? Whose standards of beauty am I applying to this tree? What are the implications about the quality of other trees if I call out this one as beautiful? These types of questions unhinge certainty, invite multiple perspectives, and situate your experience (and judgment) contextually.

What does reflexivity look like when we're talking about youth work and not trees? In the previous example, we might ask questions such as: *Why does frustration grab me when that one youth asks questions? What am I failing to understand about him? How might some of my coworkers respond to him? Why am I noticing the comments that some of the youth make and not those of others? How are race, gender, and class influencing what I notice, how I feel, and how I respond?* As you can see, reflexivity goes beyond merely thinking about an event or interaction; rather, it is an introspective process of examining what we do, what we know, and how we show up to the work. Unlike reflection, reflexive questions are relational—they invite multiple perspectives. Furthermore, because reflexivity questions assumptions and certainty, it holds the possibility of transformational change.

There are other reasons taking up a reflexive practice is essential to a narrative approach. Examining how your values, attitudes, and assumptions make their way into your practice, as well as what their effects are, is an act of accountability. Attending to these concerns helps you come into alignment with relational responsibility and an ethic of care (Paré, Richardson, & Tarragona, 2009). If we fail to ask ourselves questions that help us deconstruct what we do and don't do, we run the risk of participating in and perpetuating normative judgments and systems of dominance. Indeed, an unequivocal theme of this book is to question assumptions and expose dominant power relations. As I said earlier, this doesn't stop and start with our direct conversations with young people; it's an ongoing process of personal/professional improvement that is requisite for ethical and responsive youth work.

## From Reflection to Reflexive: Putting Yourself in Check

It's critical to recognize your assumptions.

*Eli, a youth worker*

In moving from reflection to reflexivity, we ask ourselves critical questions about how we experience the world and our assumptions about this experience. Reflexivity requires you to entertain doubt about your own perspectives.

In the activity that follows, reflect on a recent experience you've had. You could reflect on a movie, a walk you took, an interaction among people you witnessed in a public space, or a discussion you were part of with friends. Consider the following questions for reflection:

- What did you notice?
- What happened?
- What was that like?
- What do you think about it?
- How do you feel about it?
- What stood out for you that was interesting or important about it?

These reflection questions focus your attention on the event or experience—that is the object of inquiry. Even when you respond to questions about your thoughts and feelings, the thoughts and feelings are about the experience; they describe your perspective.

To move from reflection to reflexivity, turn your attention *back* to your reactions, thoughts, and feelings, and *question those*. Reflexive questions invite other perspectives, challenge assumptions, contextually situate your perspective, and interrogate power relations. In a nutshell, it's a practice of deconstructing your responses to something in order to make visible other possible constructions. Below are some general questions that invite you to take a reflexive stance.

- Am I sure about this?
- What makes me so sure?
- What discourses, institutions, or persons would support this certainty?
- What people and communities are included in my understanding and which are excluded?
- How did I come to understand this in this way?
- What are other ways to understand this?
- What other (or whose) perspectives could I consider?
- How does my social location (gender, class, sexuality, race, ability, age, ethnicity, religion, etc.) influence my reactions and interpretation of this?
- What assumptions are behind my reactions and ideas about this? What discourses do these assumptions reflect?
- How do my personal experiences and preferences influence how I see this?
- What are the effects of how I understand this on other people?

Hopefully, the distinction between reflection and reflexivity is becoming clear. The questions we ask from each position and the kinds of responses they elicit are qualitatively different from one another. Reflection can serve as a jumping-off point to asking critically reflexive questions. Taking a reflexive stance facilitates the praxis introduced earlier in Part II of this book. As White notes (J. White, 2007), this integration of knowing, doing, and being creates a space of convergence where theory and practice meet and hold the possibility of transformational change. If we fail to engage reflexively with what we (think we) know and how we show up to *do* youth work, we lose that possibility.

## Deliberate Practice: Doing Your Homework

> I have to work to keep myself from being on autopilot.
>
> *Val, a youth worker*

You may be wondering, *when do I do this reflexive questioning?* One way to answer this is to say, all the time! A critical narrative youth work practice and constructionist philosophy is very much a way of being in the world. This means that we are always checking ourselves—questioning the meanings we make and the conclusions we draw about everything. Another way to answer

---

### #FergusonSyllabus Question

Doing youth work with young people living on the borders of society and suffering the effects of systemic oppression runs the risk of reproducing normative judgments and furthering their marginalization. We all show up with our own worldview and lived experiences that leave us holding assumptions about how the world works and what that looks like in regard to gender, class, race, ethnicity, ability, sexuality, nationality, family structures, and other matters of identity.

How can taking a reflexive stance support your work with marginalized youth? What are some particular things you "know" that you might entertain uncertainty about? What will the young people you work with notice that's different when you take up a reflexive position?

---

is to break it down into when you're doing youth work with young people, and when you're not. Recall from Chapter 5 the concept of the inner dialogue. Central to a narrative approach to youth work is being reflexive *while in conversation*. That's where our inner dialogue comes in. While you're in conversation, you're engaged reflexively with your inner dialogue and other critical questions.

But cultivating a reflexive practice—one intended to help us constantly improve the quality of our practice—also requires you to intentionally make and take time to ask yourself critical questions outside of the conversational moment. It requires that you make and take time to learn and practice specific skills that you want to improve (e.g., double listening, asking externalizing questions, or building relationships). When we intentionally work on a specific skill in order to improve our practice, we engage in *deliberate practice*.

There is an entire body of literature on deliberate practice and how to achieve excellence that cuts across professions and industries (Ericsson, 2006; Ericsson, Krampe, & Tesch-Römer, 1993; Ericsson, Roring, & Nandagopal, 2007). Ericsson, Krampe, and Tesch-Römer (1993) coined the term *deliberate practice* to describe a method of improving individual performance through repeated focus on and practice of a specific skill. Within the field of youth work, Walker and Walker (2012), and Ross, Capra, Carpenter, Hubbell, and Walker (2016), for example, promote the use of deliberate practice as a method for youth worker professional development.

Deliberate practice involves four characteristics. First, deliberate practice is a method for achieving self-improvement. Learners identify a goal for themselves and create a plan to develop the skills to meet the goal. The second characteristic is repetitive practice. Learners repeat each specific skill until they master it. Third, this intentional, repetitive practice is followed by immediate feedback by someone who is knowledgeable and skilled in the area being practiced.

Finally, deliberate practice requires effort, concentration, and motivation. It isn't necessarily fun in and of itself... unless you're kind of a nerd like I am.

For example, as a narrative practitioner, I have spent hours and hours practicing questions. Because I work with a lot of queer and transgender youth and I'm interested in queer theory, I have structured deliberate practice activities to improve my ability to ask questions that deconstruct the gender binary and other heteronormative and homonormative assumptions. I practice by writing questions (or speaking them into the voice memo recorder on my phone). I also write down things that queer and trans youth say about their experiences of gender, sexuality, and identity, and write (or speak) at least three deconstructive questions to ask in response to each comment. For feedback, I show my questions to a friend who is fluent in narrative practice and queer theory. I take his feedback and rewrite some of the questions to reflect the adjustments he suggests. Believe me, this takes effort and motivation because even for a nerd, it isn't always fun.

What are some other ways to engage in deliberate practice? Andrea describes how she engages in deliberate practice to improve her responsiveness to the young people she works with in an after-school enrichment program:

> I think about the things I don't do well not as "weaknesses" or "deficits" but as opportunities for growth. This helps me not take it personally when I don't connect with a youth or they give me some hard feedback. I remind myself I don't know everything.
>
> I take notes on difficult moments—when I can't reach a youth, or I feel frustrated, or they get frustrated... anything where there's a rough spot. I take these notes throughout the week for everything that doesn't go well. I organize them by themes, looking for things that reoccur as areas I need to improve on. I choose one to focus on in supervision. I write down the whole situation without my feelings or editorializing—I just try to describe it. I bring that to supervision. In supervision, we talk about it and brainstorm other things to say or ways to approach the situation. We agree to a plan—something specific for me to work on to address that area. Maybe it's a way to approach a youth, or a question to ask them. I try it out over the next week, take notes, and come back to supervision to review it.
>
> I also talk to or watch my colleagues who are good at what I'm having a hard time doing. Having a community of learners where I can watch others work who do something better than I do it, someone with a growth mindset, is really important to me and helps me get excited to learn and get better. If you don't want to work at it, if you can't connect self-improvement and skill development back to the work, you should ask yourself, "why are you here?"

If that sounds like a lot of work, that's because it is a lot of work. Why would anyone do this? At the risk of being accused of deflecting, I'd ask: *why doesn't* everyone *do it?* Deliberate practice is what separates the average performer in any field from those who excel. In youth work as in most other areas, we often talk about people who are "naturals." In other professions that center on relationships like youth work does, we hear the people who are considered "the best" described as having "good instincts" or "intuition," or as "just a natural at it." By now, nearing the end of a book espousing anti-essentialist, constructionist ideas, you should be fairly skeptical of anything that promotes the notion that the knowing, doing, and being of youth work is located *inside* certain youth workers. These are not innate qualities. If they were, why are you even reading a book that's supposed to offer ideas about how to be a better youth worker?

---

### Reflexivity and Deliberate Practice as a Political Act

Below is one of my favorite quotes from French philosopher, Michel Foucault. Although he is referring to the work of an intellectual, I see it as an entreaty to all citizens interested in a just world, free from normative limitations and unquestioned adherence to the rules of authority. I also see it as a maxim for a reflexive and deliberate practice in service of socially just youth work. What do you think?

"The work is… to re-examine evidence and assumptions, to shake up habitual ways of working and thinking, to dissipate conventional familiarities, to re-evaluate rules and institutions and to participate in the formation of a political will" (Foucault, 1988, p. 265).

---

Indeed, I'd say that most of us think about or talk about wanting to do what we do better, but we often fall short of doing anything about it. Or, perhaps I should say, we do something, but only up to a certain point. We go to a workshop, run a tough conversation by our supervisor or colleagues, or read a book on youth work. And then we move on, without really digging in and cultivating our craft. When furthering our skills becomes especially challenging, time consuming, or tedious, it's a lot easier (certainly more fun!) to switch on Netflix or pop in some earbuds and get lost in your favorite jams. If this is you, you're not alone. I'm often there with you on the couch, and Ericsson's research on excellence and deliberate practice says that's the case for most people in most fields. Whether elite athlete, world-class surgeon, famous artist, chess master, highly effective therapist, A-list pop star, or expert engineer, the one thing that distinguishes those who eclipse others in their fields is that they *work their asses off.*

Ultimately, committing to a reflexive deliberate youth work practice is an ethical matter. It is an ethical matter to dedicate yourself to checking yourself and your assumptions, lest you impose and perpetuate oppressive and normative judgments. It is an ethical matter to devote yourself to improving your ways of knowing, doing, and being because to do any less would be a failure to live into the relational responsibility and ethic of care the youth we stand alongside deserve.

## Summary

Reflexive and deliberate practice extends the curiosity and critical questioning that are cornerstones of a narrative approach beyond the borders of our engagements with young people. Answering the invitation to interrogate assumptions and develop practice skills is a dimension of ethical practice in as much as it positions youth workers to show up with less certainty—thus making room for more perspectives—and more ways of responding to young people and the myriad concerns and possibilities that emerge in their lives.

No one can say that this is easy. Reflexivity requires both humility and the confidence to acknowledge that your understanding and way of responding isn't the only way, and maybe not the best way in any particular situation. Deliberate practice is just that: an intentional exercise and application of particular skills, done with careful attention and repetitive rehearsal. It's not for everyone. It's for those who strive to do the best possible youth work hard work can deliver.

## Highlights

| Reflection | Reflexivity |
|---|---|
| Outward focus onto something else | Focus back onto our reactions/responses |
| Individualistic | Relational/multiple perspectives |
| Thinking about | Critical thinking |
| Describing | Questioning |
| Unchallenged assumptions, certainties | Challenge assumptions, entertain doubt |
| Unsituated | Situated/contextual |
| Static | Transformational |

## Key Terms

1. **Reflection:** Reflection involves engaging in an inner dialogue or thinking about an event, interaction, person, etc.
2. **Reflexivity:** Reflexivity involves engaging in an inner dialogue that considers alternative interpretations or understandings and alternative forms of action. Reflexivity involves a stance of uncertainty (perhaps even humility) as a process in which people entertain doubts about their own knowledge or certainty about a situation, interaction, etc.
3. **Deliberate practice:** Deliberate practice is used to improve one's performance in any given field through repeated, focused practice on specific skills.

## Discussion Questions

1. How do you already take a reflexive stance in your work? What are some things you've "known" that you've entertained uncertainty about? What did that make possible?
2. What would be some areas that you can be more reflexive about? How is this important to your development as a youth worker? What has kept you from doing this? What will help you take up reflexivity in this area?
3. Identify a very specific skill you would like to be better at. Why is it important to you to improve your skill with this? How do you hope it will make a difference in your practice? What is one very specific deliberate practice exercise you can do to improve this skill? Who will be your coach or teacher to give you feedback?

## Notes

1 Quoted in: Felner, J. (2008). Woman of the year. In M. T. García (Ed.), *A Dolores Huerta Reader*. Albuquerque: University of New Mexico Press.
2 Quoted in: Marriott, M. (1997, November 13). At Home with: bell hooks; The Eye of the Storm. *New York Times*.

# 11

# FIGHT THE SYSTEM

## Critical and Political Conversations Beyond the Drop-in, Rec Center, and Squat

We need, in every community, a group of angelic troublemakers. Our power is in our ability to make things unworkable. The only weapon we have is our bodies. And we need to tuck them in places so wheels don't turn.

*Bayard Rustin*[1]

The best youth workers are always in trouble with management.

*Jena B., a youth worker*

As I stated in the introduction, my intention for this book is to bridge the gap between youth workers' understanding of systems of oppression and their everyday conversations with young people. Situating youth work in discourse, attending to operations of power, and centering youth knowledges allow youth workers to conversationally close that divide and bring to life their critical and political analyses of the world that directly impacts young people.

In this chapter, I invite you to think beyond the ostensible bounds of your work with young people and to consider ways to engage with the political and social change worlds of organizing and activism. My intention is not to compile in one chapter everything you need to know about youth organizing and activism—that is certainly an entire book for someone other than myself to write. Rather, I hope to introduce you to some possibilities by sharing ways that youth workers engage young people in social change activities.

### Why Go There? Taking Our Work to the Political World

I don't want to put band-aides on bullet wounds.

*Marjaan, a youth worker*

You've probably noticed throughout this text that I've hammered home this idea: avoid the burden of individualism and the privatization of social problems. From externalization, to the #FergusonSyllabus questions, to a post-structural analysis of power, the ideas and practices that make up a narrative approach are all about the relationship between youth's individual stories and the cultural stories that circulate through discourse.

But is it enough to honor a young woman's anger as a protest against the injustice of misogyny? When you support a black youth in creating art that is an expression of his dignity in the face of the humiliation of racism, is your work complete? What does it mean if a young person falls in love with gardening during a youth farm summer program, but goes home to a food desert? What else can you do as a baseball coach in an economically ravished rural area beyond inspiring confidence and teaching the importance of teamwork?

In other words, *is it enough to provide young people opportunities to experience agency and competence, and to imagine possibilities, if you aren't working with them to make new worlds where those possibilities may come to be?*

This is an ethical question and my answer is, *no, it's not enough.* Our work does not end when we hop on our bike or get in our car and go home. We can't claim to practice discursive, relational, justice-doing youth work if we limit our efforts to the "micro" level of engagement. When we locate problems in the social world of discourse, we need to look at the institutions that perpetuate normative specifications through policy and access to funding that impact young people, their families, and the communities they live in. Indeed, social construction insists that "we constantly consider broader contexts in which to act" (Tilsen, 2013, p. 102).

Does this mean youth workers should stop doing what they do? My answer again is, *no.* Youth workers *can and should* provide young people opportunities for dignity, pride, confidence, competence, discovery, fun, and joy. This isn't an either/or; it's a both/and: continue to provide the experiences, opportunities, and relationships for young people that make youth work meaningful, while also recognizing the need to think bigger and look further than the relationships in front of you. This is not a question of whether or not we do youth work; it's a question about the contexts in which we do youth work. This is the difference between first order change and second order, or transformational, change.

*First order change* involves acting within an existing structure or worldview. First order change maintains and sustains the existing systems. Thus, we can "empower" girls and young women to feel valuable in a culture that devalues them; instill pride in black youth in a world that dehumanizes them; teach young people to grow vegetables in the summer while year-round their families have limited access to healthy food; and we can facilitate a fun and supportive team experience for youth who see little possibility for themselves in the communities they call home. In all of these examples, the conditions have stayed the same, although some responses may have changed.

*Second order change* involves acting on the existing rules and structures that uphold a worldview or system. This change requires imagining beyond the taken-for-granted assumptions of existing worlds. For example:

- Instead of asking, *"how do we empower girls and young women to feel good about themselves in the face of misogyny?"* we ask, *"how can we build a world that values all genders and is free of misogyny and gender-based violence?"*
- Instead of asking, *"how can we encourage self-expression and self-worth among black youth?"* we ask, *"how do we dismantle white supremacy and the school-to-prison pipeline?"*
- Instead of asking, *"how can we teach gardening to youth?"* we ask, *"how do we eliminate food deserts and realize food justice and security for all communities?"*
- Instead of asking, *"how can we bring recreation opportunities to impoverished rural communities?"* we ask, *"how do we eliminate poverty everywhere?"*

Second order change is *transformational change*, change that undoes and up-ends the most basic premises of the guiding cultural meta-narratives that lead us to believe what is and isn't possible. Transformational change requires imagination and analysis, hopefulness and hard work, vision and application, and organization and flexibility. This is change from which new worlds emerge.

For youth workers, embracing transformational change also requires an acknowledgement that often *youth work occurs within systems that don't want second order change.* In fact, for the social service agencies that house many youth work programs to support transformational change, they would need to be in support of creating change that makes them obsolete. That is, these agencies and services would have to be in the business of working themselves out of business. This doesn't mean that youth work becomes obsolete; on the contrary, it means that it becomes liberated from the constraints of the social-service-industrial-complex. Such liberation would signal a seismic shift that disrupts the role of social services and charity within capitalism.

---

### #FergusonSyllabus Question

What new worlds are you compelled to imagine? What questions would you ask youth that might invite them to imagine new worlds?

## Expanding the Conversation: Taking it to the Streets

I want to challenge the whiteness in youth policy and education.

*Sunnie, a youth worker*

What does it look like when youth and youth workers work for social transformation? What are some ways that youth workers take action to effect change and do justice in the political structures that impact youth? Here are some examples of the systems change work done by some of the youth workers you've been hearing from throughout this book:

1.  *I'm not interested in charity, I'm interested in social justice and solving problems that face youth, such as homelessness and white supremacy. Youth need pathways to be in service. They are the experts, let's treat them as experts. The purpose of youth work is not to colonize or dominate, it's to liberate. This is why I do this work—to fight for another world.*

    *Marjaan, a youth worker*

    Marjaan was part of a community group organizing a forum for mayoral candidates. He created a youth panel that participated in the creation of the forum. As a staff member of a transitional living program and drop-in for youth, he also collaborated with the youth to bring their concerns to the forum. Marjaan held conversations with the young people to discuss the election and solicit their ideas about what issues they thought the candidates should speak to. He made a poster titled, *"If you could ask the mayor a question, what would it be?"* where youth wrote questions on post-its. Marjaan curated their questions for the forum so that the moderator was sure to ask them. He provided transit tokens for young people who wanted to attend the forum. Marjaan and the organizers prioritized the youth in attendance who wanted to ask a question directly of the candidates.

2.  *My intention as a youth worker is to push youth to understand they have power in their lives and in the world through personal agency, self-confidence, and self-care. When you have personal agency, you can step into responsibility, not only for yourself, but for others as well. This means taking on systems, and systems will function until they're interrupted.*

    *Eli, a youth worker*

    Eli facilitated a group for high school students interested in learning about power and privilege, and how they could become involved in their community. The youth wanted to exercise greater responsibility and agency in their school and they began to question the presence of School Resource Officers (SROs).[2] Eli asked the group, "who do you see enforcing safety in the schools—who

breaks up fights?" The youth identified teachers, counselors, and administrators as the adults they saw getting involved when there was a conflict or
safety concern, not SROs. When asked what the role of the SROs was, the
youth initially thought the officers were fairly benign. This didn't make
any sense to them—why have SROs if they don't do anything? As the
youth considered what they knew about how power operates, they began
to view the presence of the SROs as a function of a system that sought to
control young people, rather than see them as responsible. They also identified ways that they felt watched by SROs, and how this led them to cen-
sor or edit their behaviors.[3] This was especially true for students of color.
Through their observations at school and analysis in group, the students
decided to join with other organizers who were actively challenging the
school board to eliminate SROs in the public schools. They began attending school board meetings, meeting with individual board members, and
organizing other students, parents, and community members to call for the
removal of police from the schools.

3.   *Youth know better than we do what it will take to change systems because they've
     experienced them and know what doesn't work. Programs have a better chance of
     youth buy-in when youth know other young people contribute to program develop-
     ment. How do we tap youth for program development? We ask them questions that
     help them articulate and envision their needs and interests. These are questions about
     what they bring now, not just in the future. This isn't "when you grow up" or "kids
     are our future" stuff. This isn't token input. Youth who believe they have nothing to
     offer become adults who believe they have nothing to offer.*

                                                                *Emily, a youth worker*

Emily works in a youth-led organization that challenges and seeks to
transform conventional institutional structures that maintain a hard line
between staff and youth. Her program features a youth advisory board.
The agency pays the youth members and provides training and support
for them, just as it does for the adult staff members of the management
team. The youth make program and policy decisions, including those related to contracts and funding, and have direct access to the executive
leadership of the organization. For example, the rapid rehousing program
for queer and trans youth run by the agency is the brainchild of queer
youth who identified culturally specific housing as a need and brought
this to management. Youth served as consultants advising the creation of
the program.

These examples take the common refrain, "youth are experts in their own
lives" and demonstrate what it looks like when youth workers and programs

legitimately put their money where their mouth is. When youth workers honor and privilege young people's knowledge and lived experiences, youth and their stories become resources for meaningful systems change. Youth workers facilitate this amplification of young people's voices using the same concepts and practices put forth in the previous pages: attention to positioning and power relations, relational response-ability and honoring of local ethics, and a conversational practice characterized by curiosity and thoughtful inquiry.

## Summary

I began this book during the last few months of President Barack Obama's tenure in the White House and I finished it during the first few months of the Trump administration. The transition from one president to another has led to (and reflects) a dramatic cultural shift. I hesitate to call this shift one of the second order... yet. I do know this: every young person and every youth worker I've come in contact with since the 2016 election feels the difference—they *live* the difference. Everything that youth and youth workers alike had to endure and navigate before January 2017—police violence, rape culture, homo- and trans-phobia, economic oppression, nativism, islamophobia, and various practices of disenfranchisement—got amped up in the political sea-change that's abolished protections for vulnerable communities, defunded services, moved to further privatize education, and scoffed at the notion of health care as a human right. Even if you do youth work with well-resourced young people who walk the world with many privileges, there is little chance that the conditions of the political world will have no bearing on you, your work, the organization you work for, the young people you serve, their families, and the communities they live in.

My consultations with youth workers and agency staff focus now more than ever before on how to respond to young people responding to the shifting landscapes around them. Every conversation I have with youth features more fear and uncertainty—fear that their very lives are at risk from the most lethal expressions of oppression, and uncertainty conveyed through questions about the future. One youth, heartsick about the effects of climate change asked me: *will there even be a world for me?*

Although these may sound like laments of hopelessness, it is in those questions that I find hope. Perhaps, apropos to the heartbeat of this book, I should say: *I hear the possibility of a story that we can make about hope in those questions.* Why even ask if there is no concept of hope, no history with hope, or no interest in sparking hope (remember the absent but implicit)? Thus, in those questions, I also hear a call to action. I hear an urgent invitation to conversations that are bigger than the conversations we often have with youth: bigger in scope, bigger in reach, bigger in imagining a new world. I hear, in those questions posed by young people looking at the imperfect world we've handed them, a vision of transformation. Are you hearing it, too?

## Highlights

| First Order Change | Second Order Change |
| --- | --- |
| Changes occur within the system | Changes occur to the system |
| Maintains logic of system | Defies logic of system |
| Upholds/doesn't question underlying assumptions of system | Disrupts/questions assumptions of system |
| Solutions sustain system | Solutions create new system |

## Key Terms

1. **First order change:** First order change is a change within a system that maintains the structure, rules, and perspective of the system. First order change does not involve changing the context that produced the problem or concern that is the focus of change.
2. **Second order change:** Second order change is change to the system, its rules and structures, such that the context that produced the need for change is transformed.
3. **Transformational change:** Transformational change is second order change.

## Discussion Questions

1. If you had read this chapter first, how would your reaction to the idea that youth work should involve system change been the same or different from your reaction having read it at the end of the book? How do you account for this?
2. What are some examples of first order and second order change in your own life?
3. What do you want to ask young people about in order to understand their ideas for transforming the systems that affect them?

## Notes

1 Quoted in the film: Kates, N. (Producer), & Kates, N. (Director). (2003). *Brother Outsider: The Life of Bayard Rustin* [Motion Picture]. Boston, MA: PBS.
2 SROs are police officers placed in schools ostensibly to help maintain school safety and discipline by providing a police "presence" and making relationships with students. Critiques and concerns around SROs include their role in the school-to-prison pipeline and the criminalization of students of color.
3 This is what Foucault would call being under the "gaze" of authority. Foucault called the students response of self-censoring self-subjugation.

# REFERENCES

Adorno, T. W. (1991). *The Culture Industry: Selected Essays on Mass Culture*. London, UK: Routledge.

Adorno, T. W., & Horkheimer, M. (1979). *Dialectic of Enlightenment*. London, UK: Verso.

Anderson, H. (2007). The heart and spirit of collaborative therapy: The philosophical stance—"A way of being" in relationship and conversation. In H. Anderson & D. Gehart (Eds.), *Collaborative Therapy: Relationships and Conversations That Make a Difference* (pp. 41–59). New York, NY: Routledge.

Anderson, H., & Goolishian, H. (1992). The client is the expert: A not-knowing approach to therapy. In S. McNamee & K. J. Gergen (Eds.), *Therapy as Social Construction* (pp. 25–39). Los Angeles, CA: Sage.

Ang, A. (1996). *Living Room Wars: Rethinking Media Audiences for a Postmodern World*. New York, NY: Routledge.

Bakhtin, M. (1981). *The Dialogic Imagination*. Austin, TX: University of Texas Press.

Bakhtin, M. (1984). *Problems of Dostoevsky's Poetics*. Minneapolis, MN: University of Minnesota Press.

Baldwin, J. (1972). *No Name in the Street*. New York, NY: Vintage Books.

Barker, C. (2012). *Cultural Studies: Theory and Practice* (4th ed.). Los Angeles, CA: Sage.

Bateson, G. (1980). *Mind and Nature: A Necessary Unity*. New York, NY: Bantam Books.

Bavelas, J. B., Coates, L., & Johnson, T. (2000). Listeners as co-narrators. *Journal of Personality and Social Psychology, 79*(6), 941–952.

Bein, A. (2008). *The Zen of Helping: Spiritual Principles for Mindful and Open-Hearted Practice*. Hoboken, NJ: Wiley.

Brown, C., & Agusta-Scott, T. (2007). *Narrative Therapy: Making Meaning, Making Lives*. Thousand Oaks, CA: Sage.

Burr, V. (2003). *Social Constructionism* (2nd ed.). New York, NY: Routledge.

Butler, J. (1990). *Gender Trouble: Feminism and the Subversion of Identity*. New York, NY: Routledge.

Butler, J. (2004). *Undoing Gender*. New York, NY: Routledge.

Carey, M., & Russell, S. (2002). Externalising: Commonly-asked questions. *International Journal of Narrative Therapy and Community Work, 2*, 76–84.

Carr, W. (1987). What is an educational practice? *Journal of Philosophy of Education, 21*(2), 163–175.

Cary, M., Walther, S., & Russell, S. (2009). The absent but implicit: a map to support therapeutic enquiry. *Family Process, 48*(3), 319–331.

Christie, A. (1920). *The Mysterious Affair at Styles: A Detective Story*. New York, NY: Grosset & Dunlap.

Coates, L., & Wade, A. (2007). Language and violence: Analysis of four discursive operations. *Journal of Family Violence, 22*(7), 511–522.

Cummings, E. E. (1938). *New Poems, from Collected Poems*. New York, NY: Harcourt Brace.

Deleuze, G., & Guattari, F. (1987). *A Thousand Plateaus: Capitalism and Schizophrenia*. Minneapolis, MN: University of Minnesota Press.

Denborough, D. (2014). *Retelling the Stories of Our Lives: Everyday Narrative Therapy to Draw Inspiration and Transform Experience*. New York, NY: Norton.

Derrida, J. (1967). *Of Grammatology*. Baltimore, MD: Johns Hopkins University Press.

Derrida, J. (1977). *Limited, Inc*. Evanston, IL: Northwestern University Press.

Derrida, J. (1978). *Writing and Difference*. Chicago, IL: University of Chicago Press.

Doty, A. (1993). *Making Things Perfectly Queer: Interpreting Mass Culture*. Minneapolis, MN: University of Minnesota Press.

Dreyfus, H. L., & Rabinow, P. (1982). *Michel Foucault. Beyond Structuralism and Hermeneutics*. Chicago, IL: University of Chicago Press.

Eko, L. (2003). Globalization and the mass media in Africa. In L. Artz & Y. R. Kamilipour (Eds.), *The Globalization of Corporate Media Hegemony*. Albany, NY: State University of New York.

Epston, D. (1998). David consults Ben. In Dulwich Centre (Ed.), *Catching up with David Epston: A Collection of Narrative Practice-Based Papers Published Between 1991 & 1996* (pp. 175–208). Adelaide, SA: Dulwich Centre Publications.

Epston, D. (1999). Co-research: The making of an alternative knowledge. In Dulwich Centre (Ed.), *Narrative Therapy and Community Work: A Conference Collection* (pp. 137–155). Adelaide, SA: Dulwich Centre Publications.

Ericsson, K. A. (2006). The influence of experience and deliberate practice on the development of superior expert performance. In K. A. Ericsson, N. Charness, P. J. Feltovich & R. R. Hoffman (Eds.), *The Cambridge Handbook of Expertise and Expert Performance* (pp. 683–704). New York, NY: Cambridge University Press.

Ericsson, K. A. (2007). An expert-performance perspective of research on medical expertise: The study of clinical performance. *Medical Education, 41*, 1124–1130.

Ericsson, K. A., Krampe, R. T., & Tesch-Römer, C. (1993). The role of deliberate practice in the acquisition of expert performance. *Psychological Review, 100*, 363–406.

Ericsson, K. A., Roring, R. W., & Nandagopal, K. (2007). Giftedness and evidence for reproducibly superior performance: An account based on the expert performance framework. *High Ability Studies, 18*, 3–56.

Feinberg, L. (1996). *Transgender Warriors: Making History from Joan of Arc to Dennis Rodman*. Boston, MA: Beacon Press.

Felner, J. (2008). Woman of the year. In M. T. García (Ed.), *A Dolores Huerta Reader*. Albuquerque, NM: University of New Mexico Press.

Fiske, J. (1989a). *Understanding Popular Culture*. London, UK: Unwin Hyman.

Fiske, J. (1989b). *Reading the Popular*. London, UK: Unwin Hyman.

Flaskas, C., McCarthy, I., & Sheehan, J. (2007). *Hope and Despair in Narrative and Family Therapy: Adversity, Forgiveness, and Reconciliation*. New York, NY: Routledge.

Foucault, M. (1965). *Madness and Civilization: A History of Insanity in the Age of Reason.* New York, NY: Random House (original work published in 1961).

Foucault, M. (1970). *The Order of Things: An Archeology of the Human Sciences.* New York, NY: Pantheon (original work published in 1966).

Foucault, M. (1973). *Birth of the Clinic: Archeology of Medical Perception.* New York, NY: Pantheon (original work published in 1963).

Foucault, M. (1977). Truth and power. In C. Gordon (Ed.), *Power/Knowledge: Selected Interviews and Other Writings 1972–1977* (pp. 109–133). New York, NY: Pantheon Books.

Foucault, M. (1978). *The History of Sexuality, Vol. 1: An Introduction.* New York, NY: Pantheon (originally published in 1976).

Foucault, M. (1982). The subject and power. In H. Dreyfus & P. Rabinow (Eds.), *Beyond Structuralism and Hermeneutics* (pp. 208–226). Chicago, IL: University of Chicago Press.

Foucault, M. (1988). The concern for truth. In L. D. Kritzman (Ed.), *Michel Foucault:Politics, Philosophy, Culture. Interviews and Other Writings, 1977–1984* (pp. 255–267). New York, NY: Routledge.

Foucault, M. (2000). *Power: Essential Works of Foucault, 1954–1984* (Vol. 3; J. Faubion, Ed.; R. Hurley, Trans.). New York, NY: The New Press.

Frances, A. (2013). *Saving Normal: An Insider's Revolt Against Out-of-Control Psychiatric Diagnosis, DSM-5, Big Pharma, and the Medicalization of Ordinary Life.* New York, NY: HarperCollins.

Freedman, J., & Combs, G. (1996). *Narrative Therapy: The Social Construction of Preferred Realities.* New York, NY: Norton.

Freire, P. (1970). *Pedagogy of the Oppressed.* New York, NY: Continuum.

Gauntlett, D. (2008). *Media, Gender, and Identity: An Introduction* (2nd ed.). New York, NY: Routledge.

Geertz, C. (1976). "From the native's point of view": On the nature of anthropological understanding. In K. Basso & H. Selby (Eds.), *Meaning in Anthropology* (pp. 221–237). Albuquerque, NM: University of New Mexico Press.

Gergen, K. J. (2009). *An Invitation to Social Construction* (2nd ed.). Thousand Oaks, CA: Sage.

Gilligan, C. (1982). *In a Different Voice: Psychological Theory and Women's Development.* Cambridge, MA: Harvard University Press.

Greenberg, G. (2013). *The Book of Woe: The DSM and the Unmaking of Psychiatry.* New York, NY: Penguin Books.

Gustines, G. G. (2015, September 22). Ta-Nehisi Coates to Write Black Panther Comic for Marvel. *New York Times.*

Hall, S. (1973). *Encoding and Decoding in the Television Discourse.* Unpublished manuscript.

Hall, S. (1981). Encoding/Decoding. In S. Hall, D. Hobson, A. Lowe, & P. Willis (Eds.) *Culture, Media, Language.* London, UK: Hutchinson.

Hall, S. (1997). Cultural identity and diaspora. In K. Woodward (Ed.), *Identity and Difference* (pp. 51–59). London, UK: Sage.

Halberstam, J. (2005). *In a Queer Place and Time: Transgender Bodies, Subcultural Lives.* New York, NY: New York University Press.

Halberstam, J. (2011). *The Queer Art of Failure.* Durham, NC: Duke University Press.

Harre, R., & Van Langenhove, L. (Eds.) (1999). *Positioning Theory: Moral Contexts of Intentional Action.* Malden, MA: Blackwell.

Hartman, L., Little, A., & Ungar, M. (2008). Narrative-inspired youth care work within a community agency. *Journal of Systemic Therapies, 27*(1), 44–58.

Hebdige, D. (1979). *Subculture: The Meaning of Style.* New York, NY: Metheun.

Hoffman, L. (2002). *Family Therapy: An Intimate History.* New York, NY: Norton.

hooks, b. (1994). *Teaching to Transgress.* New York, NY: Routledge.

Jagose, A. (1996). *Queer Theory: An Introduction.* New York, NY: New York University Press.

Johnson, A. G. (2006). *Power, Privilege, and Difference.* New York, NY: McGraw-Hill.

Kates, N. (Producer), & Kates, N. (Director). (2003). *Brother Outsider: The Life of Bayard Rustin* [Motion Picture]. Arlington, VA: PBS.

Kellner, D. (1995). *Media Culture: Cultural Studies, Identity, and Politics Between the Modern and Postmodern.* New York, NY: Routledge.

Kierkegaard, S. (1938). *The Journals of Søren Kierkegaard* (A. Dru, Trans.). London, UK: Oxford University Press.

Kouri, S. (2015). The canonical self and politicized praxis: A tracing of two concepts. *International Journal of Child, Youth and Family Studies, 6*(4), 595–621.

Krish, I. (2010). *The Emperor's New Drug: Exploding the Anti-Depressant Myth.* New York, NY: Basic Books.

Little, A., Hartman, L., & Ungar, M. (2007). Practical applications of narrative ideas to youth care. *Relational Child & Youth Care Practice, 20*(4), 37–41.

Maalouf, A. (2000). *On Identity.* London, UK: Routledge.

Madigan, S. (2011). *Narrative Therapy.* Washington, DC: APA.

Madsen, W. C., & Gillespie, K. (2014). *Collaborative Helping: A Strengths Framework for Home-Based Services.* Hoboken, NJ: Wiley.

Marriott, M. (1997, November 13). At Home with: bell hooks; The Eye of the Storm. *New York Times.*

McEwen, J. (2017). The momentary hap of bother. *International Journal of Narrative Therapy and Community Work,* (3), 46–59.

McNamee, S. (1996). Therapy and identity construction in a postmodern world. In D. Gordin & T. R. Lindlof (Eds.), *Constructing the Self in a Mediated World* (pp. 141–155). London, UK: Sage.

McNamee, S. (2000). The social poetics of relationally engaged research: Research as conversation. In K. Deissler & S. McNamee (Eds.), *Philosophy in Therapy: The Social Poetics of Therapeutic Conversation* (pp. 146–156). Heidelberg, Germany: Carl Auer Systeme Verlag.

McNamee, S. (2009). Postmodern psychotherapeutic ethics: Relational responsibility in practice. *Human Systems, 20*(2), 55–69.

McNamee, S. (2015). Ethics as discursive potential. *Australian and New Zealand Journal of Family Therapy, 36*(4), 419–433.

McNamee, S., & Gergen, K. (1999). *Relational Responsibility: Resources for Sustainable Dialogue.* Thousand Oaks, CA: Sage.

Monk, G., & Winslade, J. (2013). *When Stories Clash: Addressing Conflict in Narrative Mediation.* Chagrin Falls, OH: Taos Institute.

Monk, G., Winslade, J., & Sinclair, S. (2008). *New Horizons in Multicultural Counseling.* Thousand Oaks, CA: Sage.

Monroe, A., Reynolds, V., & Playmondon, R. (2013). Protected: Lessons from self-organising shelter communities: 'We were already a community and you put a roof over us'. *International Journal of Narrative Therapy and Community Work,* (2), 61–78.

Morgan, A. (2000). *What is Narrative Therapy? An Easy–to-Read Introduction.* Adelaide, AU: Dulwich Centre Publications.

Morrison, Toni. (commencement speech at City College), quoted in: (No byline). (1988, May 28). Commencement. *New York Times.*

Noddings, N. (1984). *Caring: A Feminine Approach to Ethics and Moral Education.* Berkeley, CA: University of California Press.

Nylund, D. K. (2000). *Treating Huckleberry Finn: A New Narrative Approach to Working with Kids Diagnosed with ADHD.* San Francisco, CA: Jossey-Bass.

Nylund, D. (2007). Reading Harry Potter: Popular culture, queer theory, and the fashioning of youth identity. *Journal of Systemic Therapies, 26*(2), 13–24.

Paré, D. A. (2013). *The Practice of Collaborative Counseling and Psychotherapy: Developing Skills in Culturally Mindful Helping.* Los Angeles, CA: Sage.

Paré, D. A., Richardson, B., & Tarragona, M. (2009). Watching the train: Mindfulness and inner dialogue in therapist skills training. In S. Hick (Ed.), *Mindfulness and Social Work* (pp. 76–91). Chicago, IL: Lyceum Books.

Parker, I. (2007). *Revolution in Psychology: Alienation to Emancipation.* London, UK: Pluto Press.

Pence, A., & White, J. (Eds.) (2011). *Child and Youth Care: Critical Perspectives on Pedagogy, Practice, and Policy.* Vancouver, BC: UBC Press.

Reynolds, V. (2012). An ethical stance for justice-doing in community work and therapy. *Journal of Systemic Therapies, 31*(4), 18–33.

Reynolds, V. (2014). Centering ethics in group supervision: Fostering cultures of critique and structuring safety. *International Journal of Narrative Therapy and Community Work, 1,* 1–13.

Richardson, C. (2015). The role of response-based practice in activism. In M. Hyden, D. Gadd, & A. Wade (Eds.), *Response-based Approaches to the Study of Interpersonal Violence.* London, UK: Palgrave MacMillan.

Ross, L., Capra, S., Carpenter, L., Hubbell, J., & Walker, K. (2016). *Dilemmas in Youth Work and Youth Development Practice.* New York, NY: Routledge.

Sampson, E. E. (2008). *Celebrating the Other: A Dialogic Account of Human Nature.* Chagrin Falls, OH: Taos Institute Publications (originally published in 1993).

Sanders, C. J. (1999, April). *Workshop Notes: The Poetics of Resistance.* Paper presented at The Centre for Peace, "New Narratives" workshop, sponsored by The Vancouver School of Narrative Therapy, Vancouver, BC.

Sanders, C. J. (2007). A poetics of resistance: Compassionate practice in substance misuse therapy. In C. Brown & T. Augusta-Scott (Eds.), *Narrative Therapy: Making Meaning, Making Lives* (pp. 59–76). Thousand Oaks, CA: Sage.

Sanders, C. J. (2014). *Narrative Poetics of Resistance: Towards an Aesthetics of Engagement.* (Unpublished doctoral dissertation). Tilburg University, Tilburg, the Netherlands.

Schwandt, T. (2002). *Evaluation Practice Reconsidered.* New York, NY: Peter Lang Publishing.

Searle, J. R. (1995). *The Construction of Social Reality.* New York, NY: The Free Press.

Sedgwick, E. (1990). *Epistemology of the Closet.* Berkeley, CA: University of California Press.

Skott-Myhre, H. A. (2006). Radical youth work: Becoming visible. *Child Youth Care Forum, 35,* 219–229.

Skott-Myhre, H. A. (2008). *Youth and Subcultures as Creative Force.* Toronto, ON: University of Toronto Press.

Sliep, Y. (2003). Protected: Building partnerships in responding to vulnerable children: A rural African community context. *International Journal of Narrative Therapy and Community Work,* (2), 56–66.

Stacey, K. (2001). Achieving praxis in youth partnership accountability. *Journal of Youth Studies, 4*(2), 208–231.

Tarlier, D. (2005). Mediating the meaning of evidence through epistemological diversity. *Nursing Inquiry, 12*(2), 126–134.

Tilsen, J. (2013). *Therapeutic Conversations with Queer Youth: Transcending Homonormativity and Constructing Preferred Identities.* Lanham, MD: Rowman & Littlefield.

Tilsen, J., & Nylund, D. (2006). Organically validated treatments, worst practices, and other stuff that works with kids. In S. Madigan (Ed.), *Therapeutic Conversations 7 Conference Papers.* Vancouver, BC: TC7 Conference.

Tilsen, J., & Nylund, D. (2009). Popular culture texts and young people: Making meaning, honouring resistance, and becoming Harry Potter. *International Journal of Narrative Therapy and Community Work, 2,* 3–10.

Tilsen, J., & Nylund, D. (2016). Cultural studies methodologies and narrative family therapy: Therapeutic conversations about pop culture. *Family Process, 55*(2), 225–37.

Tilsen, J., Russell, S., & Michael. (2005). Nimble and courageous acts: How Michael become the boss of himself. *Journal of Systemic Therapies, 24*(2), 29–42.

Wade, A. (1997). Small acts of living. *Contemporary Family Therapy, 19*(1), 23–39.

Walker, J., & Walker, K. (2012). Establishing expertise in an emerging field. In D. Fusco (Ed.), *Advancing Youth Work: Current Trends, Critical Questions.* New York, NY: Routledge.

Walter, J. L., & Peller, J. E. (2000). *Recreating Brief Therapy: Preferences and Possibilities.* New York, NY: Norton.

Warner, M. (1999). *The Trouble with Normal: Sex, Politics, and the Ethics of Queer Life.* Cambridge, MA: Harvard University Press.

Watters, E. (2010). *Crazy Like Us: The Globalization of the American Psyche.* New York, NY: Free Press.

Whitaker, R., & Cosgrove, L. (2015). *Psychiatry Under the Influence: Institutional Corruption, Social Injury, and Prescriptions for Reform.* New York, NY: Palgrave McMillan.

White, J. (2007). Knowing, doing, and being in context: A praxis-oriented approach to child and youth care. *Child and Youth Care Forum, 36,* 225–244.

White, J. (2011). Re-Stor(y)ing professional ethics in child and youth care: Toward more contextualized, reflexive, and generative practices. In A. Pence & J. White (Eds.), *Child and Youth Care: Critical Perspectives on Pedagogy, Practice, and Policy* (33–51). Vancouver, BC: UBC Press.

White, J. (2015). An ethos for the times: Difference, imagination, and the unknown future of child and youth care. *International Journal of Child, Youth, and Family Studies, 6*(4), 498–515.

White, M. (1986). Negative explanation, restraint, and double description: A template for family therapy. *Family Process, 25*(2), 169–84.

White, M. (2000). *Reflections on Narrative Practice: Essays and Interviews.* Adelaide, SA: Dulwich Centre Publications.

White, M. (2005). *Workshop Notes.* Retrieved from http://dulwichcentre.com.au/wp-content/uploads/2014/01/michael-white-workshop-notes.pdf.

White, M. (2007). *Maps of Narrative Practice.* New York, NY: Norton.

White, M., & Epston, D. (1990). *Narrative Means to Therapeutic Ends.* New York, NY: Norton.

Willis, P. (1990). *Common Culture.* Milton Keynes, UK: Open University Press.

Wingard, B., Johnson, C., & Drahm-Butler, T. (2015). *Aboriginal Narrative Practice: Honouring Storylines of Pride, Strength and Creativity.* Adelaide, SA: Dulwich Centre.

Winslade, J., & Monk, G. (1999). *Narrative Counseling in Schools: Powerful and Brief.* Thousand Oaks, CA: Corwin Press.

Winslade, J., & Monk, G. (2000). *Narrative Mediation: A New Approach to Conflict Resolution.* San Franscisco, CA: Jossey-Bass.

Wittgenstein, L. (1922). *Tractatus Logico-philosophicus.* London, UK: Routledge & Kegan Paul.

Wittgenstein, L. (1953). *Philosophical Investigations* (Anscombe, G.E.M., Trans.). Oxford, UK: Blackwell.

Zimmerman, J. L., & Dickerson, V. C. (1996). *If Problems Talked: Narrative Therapy in Action.* New York, NY: Guildford.

# INDEX